T0194656

Chasing the Dream

the

Journey of a poor boy from Fiji

MAHESH P. RAJ

iUniverse

CHASING THE DREAM
JOURNEY OF A POOR BOY FROM FIJI

iUniverse books may be ordered through booksellers or by contacting:

iUniverse
1663 Liberty Drive
Bloomington, IN 47403
www.iuniverse.com
1-800-Authors (1-800-288-4677)

ISBN: 978-1-5320-8101-9 (sc)
ISBN: 978-1-5320-8279-5 (hc)
ISBN: 978-1-5320-8102-6 (e)

Library of Congress Control Number: 2019913548

Print information available on the last page.

iUniverse rev. date: 02/18/2020

Introduction

In December 1947, a baby boy was born weighing less than 4lbs, in the small village of Kasavu Nausori, in the Fiji Islands.

The Fiji Islands is a country in the South Pacific. It is made up of more than 300 islands. Within Fiji, there is a very large East Indian population. Their history and heritage have always posed many questions. How did they get to Fiji? We know they're from India, but exactly what part of India are they from?

The East Indians from Fiji have mostly descended from labourers from districts of the central and eastern parts of Uttar Pradesh, a Province of India. They were brought to Fiji by British Colonial rulers between 1879-1916 to work on sugar cane plantations.

After five years of hard work, these labourers were given the choice of returning to India at their own expense or to remain in the Fiji Islands.

The type of work these labourers endured was very strenuous and demanding. It wasn't just the men who had to work the fields, the women were put to work too. Even mothers, they would have to tie their babies on their back and work in the plantation all day, and then afterwards prepare food for their families. This boy's mother was no different, she tied her baby on her back, and worked all day on the plantation.

No one in the family thought this baby would survive. He was born premature, and very weak. There wasn't enough milk, food or medicine for the baby. His parents didn't know what to do, so they turned to the one thing they thought could help. As devout Hindus, they knew they could turn to their Gods for help. The baby's parents hoped that naming their son after a God would help him survive, because this God would protect their baby. They named him after a form of Shiva. Shiva is the destroyer and creator of the world in Hinduism. They didn't name the baby "Shiva" but instead another name that's associated with this great God, or "Maha" 'Esh". They picked him because they thought that he would protect the baby. This was the belief for them in those days.

His mother used to feed him milk drop by drop in his mouth, because the baby was so weak, and he could not drink the milk by bottle. But after the naming ceremony, and much prayer and waiting, the baby finally started sucking the milk by himself. They finally felt that their little baby boy will be okay. He will survive. Mahesh will survive.

Early Childhood

Mahesh's brushes with death came early and often. For some reason, he's been one of the luckiest people in the world. Throughout his childhood he's had a lot of close calls when it came to deadly encounters...

When Mahesh was very young, his parents had a big tree trunk they used to cut for firewood. One day, Mahesh and his cousin, Munna were playing on the trunk at the top of a hill. Mahesh and Munna were standing on the trunk, when it started to roll. Just when it was about to go down the hill, his cousin jumped off. Mahesh wasn't quick enough and fell down the hill with the trunk. Mahesh injured himself very badly, he got a big gash on his head and under his chin. His parents were very worried about Mahesh, and knew he had to be taken to the hospital.

Mahesh's father carried him about two miles on his shoulders, then took a bus to a small town. From there, he had to catch another bus to Suva City Hospital. They waited in the hospital waiting room for two days, without eating or sleeping. Mahesh's parents could only fear the worst. The whole time they were thinking that the doctor will come and say he is no longer alive, and they couldn't save him. Luckily, the doctor came and said that they can take Mahesh home. And that they had to take extra care of him because he is very weak. The doctor advised his parents to give Mahesh something to make him stronger. So, from that day he was given cod liver oil to drink, he did not like it. It tasted bitter and gross, but he had to take it.

When he was about 5 years old, on a very hot day, Mahesh, was playing outside his house. The house was very close to a hill. While playing outside, Mahesh became very lucky again. Out of nowhere the ground and everything around him started to shake. It was the biggest earthquake to ever hit the Fiji Islands. Right outside their home, a mudslide came down the hill where Mahesh was playing and almost buried him alive. Mahesh's mom quickly ran outside and brought him inside the house. As soon as they came inside a second mudslide rolled down that hill, right where Mahesh was playing. It buried half of their home, and all of Mahesh's father's plowing and farming equipment.

By the time Mahesh was around 6 years old, he had a five-year-old brother and three and a half year old sister. They lived very simple life.

As children, they knew very little about Christmas. On Christmas Day, they would get a cold drink and a bun as their present. The type of toys they would get would be balloons and maybe a whistle. They never had Christmas cake. If they had any visitors on Christmas Day, they had a chance to have chicken dinner.

Diwali was different for them, they celebrated happily, had nice food cooked by their mom and had candlelight or homemade diya. For New Year's, they had no clue.

Mahesh always played with his friend from next door, Babu, who was also around the same age as Mahesh. One day, Babu brought Mahesh a sugarcane about two feet long, and wanted to share half of it with Mahesh. They both grabbed an end, and Mahesh was going cut it in half. Mahesh thought he would be clever, and would pull the sugar cane towards himself to get a bigger piece. So, as he swung the knife towards the cane, he yanked his end to get a slightly bigger piece.

Unfortunately, he pulled too hard and ended up cutting his friend's wrist. They both ran to their house and hid, as they thought they would be in big trouble. They couldn't hide for long, because Babu had to be taken to the hospital to be bandaged up to stop the bleeding. Later that evening, Babu's family came to their house to check up on Mahesh and make sure his father did not beat him. Those days' neighbours were like family members. Even though Mahesh cut their son, they knew it was by accident, and did not want to see Mahesh get in too much trouble for it.

Tailevu

When Mahesh became old enough to start attending school, he had to go live with his uncle in a different district called Tailevu, as there weren't any schools where Mahesh lived. His uncle also had a big family; eight children and four adults in one house. It was a small house with a leaky roof. Every time it rained the kids had to place empty pots and containers to collect the water. There were no beds for the kids to sleep on. All of the kids had to sleep on the floor, which was basically mud mixed with cow dung, that was leveled by hand. They all had to sit on this floor to have their dinner. Most of the time their dinner was rice and potato curry, or dhal. Rice for breakfast, and a packed parcel for lunch, which was always roti. Mahesh's uncle had one small house for rice storage, and for those who are non-vegetarian, they cooked chicken and fish there as well.

Eventually the kids decided to make their own beds from bush timber, and a mattress from dry grass. All the kids made their own beds and tied their mosquito net. When Mahesh's uncle and aunt were not home they would have pillow fights. The kids would name themselves after different countries. They gave Mahesh India, and India always lost the fight, but it was fun for them. There were no issues with the kids, they were all like brothers and sisters. There was only one big problem...the toilet. There was only one toilet. It's called the pit toilet, it was pretty much a hole in the ground, with four walls around it, ten to fifteen yards away from the house. If you need to go during the night, you'd have to carry a hurricane light or lantern with you. It was pretty much an outhouse.

When Mahesh's grandfather would go to the pit toilet, he would take a lot of time, usually it was because he was smoking inside. But sometimes, he would fall asleep in there. The kids thought they'd help him wake up by throwing hard mud at the outhouse. It was made of flat iron, so it made a huge sound when hit with something.

School was four miles away from Mahesh's uncle's house so they had to get up very early to make it on time. Mahesh and his cousins had to walk without shoes and carry all their books and lunch in their hands. Mahesh only needed a slate and chalk, since it was his first day of school. The first half of their journey to school was muddy and grassy; the second half was a gravel road. On rainy days their legs would become so dirty that they would have to wash them in the sewer drain. Luckily cleanup was quick, since the kids use coconut oil on their body before they go to school, so the dirt washed right off their oily legs.

In class (grade) one, students would have to sit on the floor. The "floor" is basically sand. The good news was that if you forgot your slate, you could write on the floor. When he started grade two and three Mahesh wasn't able to afford his own books. He had to use his cousin's old books. His cousins were very nice to him and some of his friends in school also helped him out by giving him pens, pencils, and other supplies because he was a bright student. The teachers liked him too, and helped with the things he could not afford, and in exchange, Mahesh would do some small work for them.

After school, all the kids would have to help on the farm, and then come home to help with cooking. Most of the time the ladies and girls did the cooking, and the boys chopped wood, and filled buckets with water from the well. It was very 1950s.

Mahesh's house in Tailevu

Mathematics Center in Tehran

Swamp Dive and Bus Story

After two years at his Uncle's house, Mahesh's brother came and joined him. His uncle and cousins built another small house; all the adults moved into that house, and all the kids lived in the old house, like brothers and sisters. The kids loved this arrangement, they hardly fought and got along really well. It was the most fun for them.

Sometimes they would go swimming in the swamp. To make sure that they wouldn't get dirty and caught, they would go swimming naked. Those days they did not wear any underwear, only shorts and t-shirt. So swimming naked meant that no one would know that they went in the swamp.

During one of these swamp swimming sessions, Mahesh had another brush with death. He was swimming and decided to dive. He dove head first in the swamp, and got his head stuck in the mud under water. He could not pull it out himself, and began to panic. Luckily his cousins were watching, and quickly pulled him out.

And that wasn't the only time he's almost gotten himself killed.

One time, they were loading hay on a sledge that was being pulled by bulls, as the hay was to be transported somewhere. As the hay was being loaded, Mahesh jumped up and sat on top of the hay. As soon as the bulls pulled the sledge, he slid in front of it, and then fell under it. Everyone thought Mahesh was going to die right then and there, but his cousin quickly stopped the bulls, and managed to pull him out from the back of the sledge. He was so lucky. He had survived the mudslide, being trapped under the tree trunk, getting his head stuck in the swamp and being trapped under the sledge. But don't worry, Mahesh wasn't always the victim.

During one school holiday Mahesh and his cousin went to his parents' house to hangout. Mahesh started playing with a cane knife, and accidentally he cut his cousin's ankle. They both ran into the house. Mahesh's mother quickly bandaged it with her kameez to stop the bleeding.

Once, when they were on their way back to Tailevu from Mahesh's parents' place after a school holiday, Mahesh's father was dropping the two kids off at a local bus stop on a main road. There was a store there, right on the three-way junction where the bus stop is. Mahesh's father asked Mahesh and his cousin to wait in the shop, and he would go on the road to stop the bus. While they were waiting in the store Mahesh saw a bus coming, so he ran out, towards the stop, to where the bus looked like it was going. He started to cross the road, but as soon as he was halfway across, the bus turned towards him. Mahesh quickly ran back and dove in the grass on the side of the road.

The bus driver and all the passengers ran out looking under the bus; everyone thought he was dead. Mahesh's father came running. He found him in the grass on the side of the road. Mahesh's father was very upset with Mahesh, and his nephew, and told them not to come out of the shop until he comes and gets them. Mahesh was shaking and sat in silence for a long time.

Because his childhood was full of very hard times, Mahesh was a skinny kid. But, he was strong and healthy. He was a fast runner, one of the fastest in his class. Although Mahesh lived a very hard childhood, he made the best of the situation he was in. In grade three, he became the captain of his soccer team. His teacher made him play the front positions, because he was a good runner.

Parents moving to Tailevu

When Mahesh was around 12 years old, his parents were having a hard time in Rewa Nausori, because a large Sugar Mill company called CSR decided to close down. Mahesh's father was growing sugar canes and supplying them to this company as his sole means of income.

The first Nausori Sugar mills were on the bank of the Rewa River. Most of the sugar cane that was transported to this mill was by punt boat. Due to bad weather it was very difficult to transport sugar, and the CSR company decided to close down this mill.

After the mill closed down, his father started to do banana farming. This farm was not successful due to weather issues and people stealing his crops. Since the banana farm was on native lease land, his father decided to move the rest of the family to Tailevu, into his brother's house where Mahesh was staying. Mahesh's uncle then moved into his new house with his family. Their new house was very close to school, and it had a river in front of it. It was a nice house with four bedrooms, but Mahesh stayed with his family. He had two brothers and two sisters, five kids, and his parents total seven. All living in the same old small house.

They started life again with not enough food and clothes for all of them. As the oldest child in the family Mahesh had to help out a lot. Since there wasn't much to eat, he had to go into the bush to get some fruit, dry coconut and Navi. Navi is like a cashew nut, just boil and eat. It wasn't sweet, so it could be eaten every day. One good thing was that they had a cow that was left by his uncle. A few of Mahesh's first jobs were to help his father milking the cow, and to fill water in the pit toilet. The well was on the other side of the house so that the well water didn't get mixed with the toilet water. Most of the time, they had to drink the well water. Every day after school, Mahesh had to help his parents on the rice farm and then come back to help his mom prepare food.

As a child, Mahesh would always sleepwalk. Some nights he would go play with the calves or start milking the cow. One night he was walking by himself to his uncle's house, and his father saw him when he was coming home from the shop where he would hang out most nights with his friends drinking grog. Luckily his father saw him and brought him home. No one saw him leave the house. When Mahesh's father and mother asked him about it, he couldn't remember anything.

The landlord on their new farm had a small shop to supply groceries and some clothes on credit, until crops were ready for harvest. After harvesting the crops, most of the money went to the landlord. The landlord deducted all of his credit first, and then paid Mahesh's father a small amount, and sometimes there would be nothing left.

Every Saturday, Mahesh's duty was to take one bottle of homemade ghee and some eggs to the Korovou town market, which was more than five miles from his house. He traded the ghee and eggs to grocery stores, for food. He had to walk down without shoes, on gravel and feeder road, carrying the groceries in a sack on his shoulder. If he had any money, he would take the bus as far as the gravel road. Mahesh was happy to do this because it made his family happy. On Saturdays they would have something different to eat.

After a few years on this farm, the family had to deal with constant flooding. This lasted for two years, destroying all the crops. Because of this, Mahesh's father did not have any money to pay for school fees. They did not understand how important school was in those days. Instead of going to school, the kids had to stay at home to help their parents on the farm. Mahesh liked it, because most of the time he played in the bush, did some fishing and helped other farmers for cash and food. During this time, he learned how to climb on the coconut trees. No matter how tall the coconut tree was, if there were coconuts on that tree Mahesh would climb it. He also spent his time swimming in the river. However, fishing was his favourite hobby, as it also helped him feed his family.

Mahesh's family was very poor, but they were honest people. Sometimes they would not have anything to eat, and Mahesh would have to go and find something from the bush. Most of the time he would catch shrimp. When he could not get any fish, he would look for some navies. Sometimes their dinner would only be navies and black tea.

Friends and Pranks

Mahesh and his friends were always up to no good. One day a man from their village complained about Mahesh climbing a very tall coconut tree, and other things he did not like Mahesh doing, like picking mangoes and navis. He would always complain to Mahesh's father, and his father would always beat Mahesh without asking. Mahesh would get beaten all the time as soon as someone complained, no questions asked. One time when his father pulled his belt out to beat him, Mahesh started laughing. When his father took his belt off, his pants dropped, and in those days, they did not wear any underwear.

Because this man was the cause of most of Mahesh's beatings, Mahesh, his brother and his two cousins decided to scare him. They knew this man very well. He was very superstitious and easy to scare. One day this man was coming home late at night. Mahesh and his friends took a hurricane lamp and climbed on top of a mango tree. When the man came close to the tree, they dropped the lamp and pulled it up again on top of the tree, as if it was floating. The man saw this and ran home. The next night, Mahesh's brother and two of his second cousins did the same thing on the next tree. As soon as the man passed the second tree they shook the branches, and one of his cousins tied grass to make him fall. The man ended up falling a few times when trying to run away. The man was very scared and ended up getting sick. People from the village started visiting him, he told everyone that he saw a ghost. He thought it was the soul of an old woman who passed away recently. When Mahesh's father heard this story, he knew that there was no ghost. He knew it must be his kids who were responsible for this. Mahesh's father called all four of them and beat them without asking any questions. He told them to not pull pranks like this anymore. That they made an old man very sick. Mahesh and his friends refused to stop giving this man and his family a hard time, because it wasn't just Mahesh this man was picking on, he was also complaining to Mahesh's friends' parents too.

One of this man's sons married a girl from the town he was working in. However, his parents would always ask him to come home and help on the farm, especially during harvesting time. Whenever he came with his wife, she refused to go to the toilet during the day, and made her husband take her at night. Everyone's toilet house is the same, they're made of flat iron, and is about ten yards away from the house. One night, when she went inside the toilet, Mahesh and his friends threw solid mud and stone to scare her. They did this so maybe they won't come to help their parents, and Mahesh and his friends would get some work for one shilling. Working all day in the farm is nothing for them, but one shilling was big money at that time.

Picnic Story

Mahesh's father was a very hard-working man, he managed to work on a dairy farm, and at the same time worked on his rice farm. Within two years, he managed to save enough money to enroll Mahesh, and one of his brothers, Sagan, and sister, Lata, back into school.

Mahesh never forgot about the time he went on a picnic from school. They did not have enough money for the picnic, so one of his teachers paid their bus fare, in exchange for one bottle of ghee. They did not have a lot of money with them. Mahesh had two shillings, which his grandfather gave him on his last visit. The picnic was in Suva City. After playing they became very hungry. His brother and sister looked to Mahesh to see if he can buy something to eat. The lunch they were provided was so small, it was like they did not eat anything at all. It was pretty much the same as the lunch they would take to school every day. Mahesh's brother went to buy three sweets for them, it did not help their hunger, but at least they had something to eat. Mahesh's brother and sister came to him and asked if he had any money. Mahesh said he had two shillings, which is 24 pennies. His sister said "really?", Mahesh replied "yes, let's go and get something to eat." They went and got one bottle of cold drink and some buns.

On their way home, Mahesh's brother asked him where he got this money. Mahesh told his brother that their grandfather gave it to him. The week before, when their grandfather came to their house, he went to the outhouse at night and dropped his flashlight in the toilet. Mahesh's grandfather called him from inside the toilet and told Mahesh what happened. His grandfather told Mahesh that if he gets the flashlight out of the toilet, he will give him one shilling. Mahesh asked for two shillings, and his grandfather agreed. Mahesh put his hand all the way in the toilet, and grabbed the torch, his chin was touching the toilet slab, but he grabbed the flashlight, gave it to his grandfather, and got his two shillings. His grandfather was so glad, because it was brand new.

When Mahesh's mom found out, she made him bathe four times. She had to bring water from the well to him. She did not want Mahesh to be close to the well, because she did not want the water to go back into the well. That's how Mahesh got two shillings. They went home happy, walking, laughing and talking to each other because they had something to eat, and they were not hungry anymore.

Mahesh's dad getting sick

About a year later, his father started getting sick. They could not afford to take him to a better hospital, just the local dispensary. Nothing was getting better, they had to sell the cow to cover some of the costs of medicine, but still his father did not feel well. The rice farming was not very profitable, since most of the money went to their landlord. His uncle and cousins decided to bring all of them to stay with them in the house they were living in.

This house was very nice, it had four bedrooms, and they converted the kitchen into another bedroom and moved the kitchen outside. This house was very close to school - it was just next door and had a river in the front. Everyone was very happy to live together. Some of the kids had to sleep in the front veranda on the floor. If there were any visitors, they had to wait until they left, then they could go to sleep.

There was a total of twenty-three people living in this house; grandfather, grandmother, uncle, aunt, nine cousins, four brothers, three sisters and his parents. Everyone staying together very happily. The kids liked each other like they were all brothers and sisters. Mahesh also liked it because the house was not leaking, it had wooden floors and was right next to the school.

Muli Chor

One Sunday evening Mahesh and some friends from school went to the cinema to watch a Hindi movie. Those days Hindi movies ran for more than three hours. After the movie, they were all walking down from Korovou Town, about three miles from their school. Along the way, they were walking, running, and scaring each other. When they came close to the school, Mahesh's neighbour's son, Dev, grabbed Mahesh's hand and started running fast. They ran right to the school compound and crossed the grounds to the back of the school into the vegetable garden. Mahesh had no idea what was on Dev's mind. Dev pulled three radishes from the garden, broke the leaf, gave one to Mahesh, and kept two for himself.

One of the teachers' cottages was behind the school garden, and his mother was sitting outside on the steps. She saw two kids come running into the garden, and then run away. She could not recognize them because it was dark. She told her son what she saw that night. The next morning, the HeadMaster wanted to know who it was, so he started investigating the matter. He found out from the other students who went to the movies that it was Mahesh and Dev who ran faster than the rest of the group. Dev was known to be a troublemaker, as he was caught stealing before. The HeadMaster came to Mahesh, and asked only one question, who took two radishes, you or him? Mahesh said it was Dev. The HeadMaster told Mahesh that he was ok to go and play.

The HeadMaster then asked a teacher to make two signs that said "muli chor" (radish thief). When the bell rang, everyone had to get in line to go inside the school. After the morning prayer, The HeadMaster called Mahesh and his friend forward, and he told the teacher to hang the signs around their necks. The HeadMaster told them that this was their punishment for stealing. They both had to stay outside in front of the driveway all day. When anyone passed them and asked about the sign, they made up a story.

At lunchtime when Mahesh's father was coming for lunch, they turned the sign around. When he asked what they were doing, Mahesh's friend quickly said they were picked to welcome a visiting teacher and education officer. That they were coming to their school this afternoon. Mahesh's father was very proud that his son was picked to welcome the visiting teacher and education officer. Later that evening, when he came to know the true story, Mahesh's father just laughed, because he understood it was Dev who made Mahesh do this.

That wasn't the only time they would steal food. One time one of Mahesh's cousins, Master, stole a bunch of bananas from the school compound. Mahesh's uncle's house was next to the school compound and there was a banana plantation on the edge of his uncle's land. Mahesh's cousin cut a bunch of bananas from the tree, ones that were just about to ripen, and hid them in the grass at the end of his farm land. When the bananas ripened, he told Mahesh and one of his brothers, whom he trusted the most, and Mahesh told his brother. The four of them ate all of the bananas within a few days. No one ever found out about this. The school committee, teachers and neighbours would never believe that Mahesh's family would do something like that.

Starting their own Rice Farm

A short time later, Mahesh's family had their own farmland next to his uncle's land. Only rice farming could be done on this land. Everyone worked on the farm together. But someone needed to be on the farm full-time. It was between Mahesh and his brother, Sagan, to decide who will work full-time on the farm. Sagan offered to leave school and work on the farm because he was stronger than Mahesh. However, his brother was also a very bright student and because he was younger, he was qualified to take the secondary school exam. Because of this, Mahesh decided to leave school and work full time on the farm.

Mahesh and Sagan were both bright students. Mahesh would always come in first on the annual exam. Only once did he come in third place, where two girls placed ahead of him. All of his cousins and friends started teasing Mahesh about coming in third. From that moment on, Mahesh always came first in his class. The girl who came in first was The HeadMaster's daughter, and the one who came in second was a school official's daughter. Not to imply that these girls cheated; they were both very bright students. But nevertheless, it was decided. Mahesh had to leave school, while his brother continued on with his studies.

One day, Mahesh's father sent him to bring a pair of bulls for ploughing land, from one of his second cousins, who lived about 40 miles away. Mahesh and his cousin took the bus and arrived at his Uncle's farm around 10:30am. After a light lunch, they started walking back home with the bulls. They had to control one bull each. Every time any vehicle passed, the bulls started running away. It was a gravel road and due to dry weather, there was a lot of dust. So when trucks passed by, they had to turn around to avoid the dust, while trying to maintain control of the bull. They had to hold the rope tightly, so the bulls wouldn't run away. It was almost midnight by the time they arrived home. Mahesh was very tired and went to bed right away. The next morning his father woke him up very early to plough the land, because they had to return the bulls as soon as they were done ploughing.

Rice and Poultry Farming

After some time, Mahesh's uncle helped them build their own house from bush timber and corrugated iron, and some material from their old house. The floor was again mud and mixed with cow dung leveled by hand, they had to do this every month. The house was on Mahesh's uncle's land, not very far from his uncle's house. Mahesh's family happily moved out, because Mahesh's oldest cousin was going to get married very soon.

Mahesh's father started getting better, and managed to find a job. In the village there was a dairy and chicken farm owned by a man named Mr. Tom Edward, which was not very far from their house. His father was hired to work in the poultry farm. This was a seven day a week job, but his father accepted it, knowing that Mahesh and his other son would help out on weekends.

Mahesh worked full time on the rice farm. He would also receive help from his cousins, and Mahesh would go and work on their farm in exchange. Finally, it seemed as though the family had some money with Mahesh's father working every day at his new job. And Mahesh was managing the rice farm well. It was all hard work, back in those days they didn't have tractors or any other machinery to plough the land. Mahesh had to use bulls to plough the land. He also had to plant the rice in the muddy field all day, which came with a lot of back pain, as he was bent over planting the rice all day. Sometimes Mahesh wouldn't get a nice meal for dinner, just sweet potatoes and black tea. Luckily for Mahesh, rice farming was seasonal, so for half of the year Mahesh had a lot of time to play soccer.

Dog Prayer

The family had a dog, it was very nice and reliable. However, when she became old, she started coughing constantly, sometimes for a very long time. The family decided that they needed to get rid of her. Mahesh's uncle told the kids to take the dog across the river and leave it there. She can go and survive in the Fijian village. Mahesh, his brother and their cousin took the dog in a bamboo craft crossing the river during full tide. As soon as they passed the river halfway, his cousin pushed the dog in the river. When the dog was swimming back to the craft, Mahesh's brother hit her in the head with an oar, and she drowned in the river.

Mahesh's 5-year-old cousin was watching them from the shore; he ran home and told his grandmother what he saw. They got in big trouble. Their Grandmother told them that it was a big sin to kill their dog. Their Grandmother arranged with a pundit to come and do a prayer for them. When the ceremony was half way over the pundit asked the kids why they arranged this prayer, and their grandmother told the pundit they accidentally killed the dog in the river.

The pundit said this is a big sin and they had to do an even bigger prayer.

The kids had to pay money separately and had to act like a dog as part of the prayer. The Pundit started doing the prayer, when he was almost done, he took his walking stick and hit their head like they did to the dog. Mahesh got mad at the pundit, because he was beaten twice in the head. He got up and almost kicked the pundit but everyone held him back.

The family also had one horse. It was a big horse. Mahesh liked to ride this horse, because she did not go that fast. Sometimes four of them would ride her at once, but she didn't like to run fast. When Mahesh or his cousins tried to make her run, she would throw them off by lifting her legs. Mahesh fell so many times but did not quit riding.

Mahesh's Brother and Education

When Sagan completed his secondary school exam, he had to move to Suva City with his cousin to complete his secondary school education. But their father wanted him to come home and work on the farm every weekend. Therefore, Sagan had to take the last bus every Sunday to get back to Suva City for work the next day. Most of the time he had to wear his uniform on Sundays too, because he did not have any extra clothes.

Because of his good marks, Mahesh's brother was able to go to one of the best schools in the city, Mahatma Gandhi High School. Due to hard times in the family, one of Mahesh's sisters did not attend any school, because she passed the school age. Lata, who did attend school, had to quit after completing primary school. Mahesh's two youngest brothers and one sister were in the primary school next to his uncle's house. They have completed their education.

Chupat and Bahilla

When you are poor, people will take advantage of you. One day, one of Mahesh's father's relatives came to his house, and asked his father, what Mahesh had been up to since rice farming season was over. "Was he learning any trade work?" This relative told Mahesh's father that he was building a new house in Suva City. He told his dad that Mahesh could come and stay at the job site, and learn some trade work. That it could be a good opportunity for Mahesh to learn.

Mahesh's father agreed and sent Mahesh to work for this relative, he thought it would be a great opportunity for Mahesh to learn some trade work. That was not the case, Mahesh was just used to do all the strenuous work, like digging a drain for foundation, or mixing concrete with a spade, or carrying bricks and gravel with the wheelbarrow. Mahesh had to stay in a small hut, without a proper bed. And at the end, when it was time to do all of the finishing, Mahesh was not required anymore.

One day, Mr. Tom Edward gave his father an offer to look after his cattle on a remote island in Fiji. Where there would be no other human beings. Absolutely no civilization, only cattle. So no school, no medical facilities, and there were no stores to purchase anything. If they needed any supplies, Mr. Edward would bring them when he would come by boat every two weeks. There were no roads or bridges to get to this island. There was no phone contact either.

Mahesh heard about this, he was very happy, because with the soccer season over, he would have a lot of time to play in the sea, and fish, whatever he wanted to do every day. But, his father refused to take the offer. Mahesh asked his father why did you refuse this offer? His father replied "Are you Chupat? Do you want to become a Bahilla?" Mahesh did not understand the words "Chupat" and "Bahilla". He never heard those words before.

Sometime passed Mahesh's uncle decided to go into the fishing business. He rented a fishing boat run by steam. They called this boat a steamer. One day Mahesh went deep sea fishing with his uncle, his two cousins and a fisherman. The fisherman was an expert on the sea, and knew the good spots where the big fish were. While they were fishing, the weather was very nice and calm. Then his older cousin jumped in a small boat; he wanted to do "trolling" fishing. All of a sudden three big waves came and the rope that tied the small boat to the steamer broke. They could not see him, he was lost in the waves. After the three big waves passed they saw him. Good thing his fishing line was tied to the steamer as he was holding on to that line. They managed to pull him back in the steamer. Mahesh's uncle was very worried and said "That's it! Let's go back. no more fishing business."

While all this was happening Mahesh kept thinking about the two words his father said to him "chupat" and "bahilla". One day, he went to his cousin that was like a best friend to him, and asked about these two words. His cousin told Mahesh that one day he'll know what it is, and that they should just go and box. He told Mahesh that if Mahesh beats him, he would explain what those words mean.

Mahesh and his cousin boxed in a small house made of flat iron. His uncle used the house for storage. Because it was made of flat iron, the house made a lot of noise when you touched it. They were boxing for a long time. Suddenly his grandmother opened the door as she thought they were fighting with each other. As soon as she opened the door, Mahesh looked towards her direction, and he was on the floor knocked out. That was the first time Mahesh saw stars in the day time.

After a few minutes, he woke up and realized his four front teeth were all loose and the colour changed to yellow. The dentist told Mahesh that he had to pull them out, or they would fall out by themselves later.

So now, Mahesh needed to get dentures. To get the dentures made, you need money and you have to go to the city. The whole family decided to help Mahesh get his dentures. Within one month's time he got them. The dentures looked very nice, Mahesh was very glad, because his teeth were sticking out before. Mahesh's parents did not ask or complain about this incident to his uncle. Nor did they ask his cousin why he hit him so hard. They all lived very friendly and they knew it was an accident.

Throughout all this, the words "chupat" and "bahilla" were still on Mahesh's mind. Continuous heavy rains destroyed all of their crops, and was making everyone, especially Mahesh, in a bad mood.

Mahesh's father was promoted to be a supervisor in the field and wanted him to take over his old job on the poultry farm. There was not much work to do their rice farm. Mahesh's father told him that this is your best opportunity to make some money. His father spoke to Mr. Edward to make sure Mahesh would get this job, and then he would take over the field supervisor's job. Mr. Edward agreed to give Mahesh a job in the poultry farm. Everyone in the field was after this position. Mahesh's father told Mahesh, make sure to be on time every day. It is a seven days a week job. So he has to be there every day to work. The duties were to clean the eggs and feed the chickens. Sometimes Mahesh got so dirty, that he had to sit away from everyone else to have his lunch because of the smell. But, he kept working. It was a little easier than working on the rice farm.

Mahesh took the job because he had felt sorry for his father. Recently, his father was trapped in a flood. There was a very heavy wind and rain storm two weeks ago due to hurricane in the ocean nearby. Mahesh's father sent everyone to his brother's house, while he stayed back in his small house all by himself. When it became dark the flood water rose. Mahesh and his cousin tried to go and bring him to his uncle's house. But, because of the very heavy rain and wind it was difficult for Mahesh and his cousin to get him. The boat was made of flat iron, so it was very difficult to control in the heavy wind. They had to leave Mahesh's father there for the night. This made Mahesh very worried, as he knew his father would be trapped in their home.

First thing the next morning, Mahesh and his cousin went to see if his father survived the night. When they got there, they were happy to see that he was on the roof. He did not know how to swim, so it was a good thing that the water didn't rise any further. Since then, if there was any rain, Mahesh's father was the first one out of the house.

Mahesh worked in the poultry farm seven days a week. When the soccer season started he didn't have any time to play soccer. He asked his father to have one day off so he can play soccer with his home team. But the answer was no.

For practice it would be okay, he got up early in the morning and went to the grounds for his soccer practice with the other players. Those days there was no coach on local teams. Everyone just got together and played. When he was selected to play for the district team, Mahesh needed to have one day off. He decided to go and see Mr. Edward by himself and explain to him that he had been selected for the district team, and the team manager needed him every Sunday in town to practice. Mr. Edward was a nice man, and allowed him the day off.

Mr. Edward told Mahesh "You do not have to be in the poultry farm all the time. Whenever you needed to leave you can go, your job is to feed the chicken and do what is to be done." Mahesh mentioned that his father may not like this, Mr. Edward replied "Your father is not your supervisor. He is in charge of field only."

This was a huge surprise and relief to Mahesh. He became so glad, now that he had lots of time to practice, and to play for his team. However, Mahesh's father knew how much other people wanted this job. So, when Mahesh needed to go out of town to play with the other district teams, his father would go into the poultry farm for the weekend. He did this because he did not want someone else to take Mahesh's job.

The words "chupat" and "bahilla" were still not going out of his mind. He went to his best cousin again. His cousin was a smart person, he had two years secondary school education. But he was working as a labourer on the farm. Or sometimes he would help a fisherman in the night, he would work for some cash or fish to feed his family. Luckily, the primary public school next to his house needed someone to teach class (grade) one. The school's committee asked Mahesh's uncle to talk to his son to help with the committee and be a teacher while they look for someone else to teach. However, since the pay was very low, his cousin refused initially. The school committee insisted that they needed help, so finally, Mahesh's cousin agreed to teach.

After accepting this job, his cousin's lifestyle changed. Everyone in the house started reading and writing. His cousin did some courses and became a full time schoolteacher. But he did not stop studying. Mahesh's cousin registered in a University-level course from Hemingway's Correspondence School of New Zealand, and also to the University of South Pacific. Mahesh would always call him, "Master".

Mahesh saw his cousin Master studying very hard every day. He did not have time to spend with him, but he stayed with him all the time. Mahesh would give him tea, water or milk when his cousin Master was studying. Most of the time he made soup from cabbage and tomatoes he collected fresh from the farm. One day his cousin Master asked Mahesh, "Why don't you do some type of course with me."

Mahesh replied, "Yeah right, with my education, what can I do?"

Then his cousin said to him, "Do you want to know the meaning of 'Chupat' and 'Bahilla'?" His cousin explained to him that 'Chupat' meant *stupid* and 'Bahilla' meant that you have no brain, no knowledge of anything, and no future. His cousin asked him, "Do you know why your father put you in the poultry farm to clean the chicken poop? Does he want you to do this all of your life?"

Then his older cousin's wife came in and said to Mahesh, "Keep cleaning Tom's eggs." This made Mahesh very upset and mad.

His cousin told him "You have a bright future." and "If you do something, just don't sit down here and disturb me."

Mahesh asked his cousin "What do you think I should do?"

Master suggested a bookkeeping course from Hemingway's Correspondence School. Mahesh told Master that he would do it, if he promises to help him. Master insisted that he do it. That Mahesh is a bright, and knowledgeable person. Mahesh asked Master to register him as he had some money. However, they had to wait until after Master's older brother's wedding, which was happening the next week. Mahesh always called this cousin, "Bro."

A week before the wedding, visitors from all over started coming. Everyone was having fun. It was a nice bright sunny day; all the kids knew how to swim went to the river for their bath. As Mahesh was diving from the shore he lost his dentures in the river. Everyone tried looking for them, but it was very hard to find the dentures. All the cousins and friends from the village were good swimmers. But since it was getting dark, it became difficult to see. Eventually, it was too dark and they could not find the dentures. Mahesh was very upset and sad, so he went home and slept. He did not want to speak to anyone without the dentures. No one ever saw him sad like this before.

The next day Bro came to him and told him to get ready, that first thing tomorrow morning they are going to go to Suva City to get his new dentures. He also helped Mahesh with some of the payment. The next day they went to the dentist, and within two days' time, Mahesh got his new dentures. His cousin Bro also brought him a new pair of shoes. The dentures fit him well. Mahesh was so glad. This was the first time he got a new pair of shoes, and a set of dentures with a piece of gold in the front.

After the wedding, once everyone left, Mahesh went back to his cousin Master regarding the Bookkeeping course. He told his cousin to forget about registering him for the course because he did not have any money left. His cousin said only two words "Chupat" and "Bahilla". Mahesh's older cousin's wife, on the other hand, could never stay silent and told Mahesh to keep cleaning Tom's eggs, which made Mahesh very upset and mad again.

The next day Mahesh's father went to Master and asked what happened to him. Why was Mahesh very sad and upset, they replied "nothing". They told him that Mahesh had spent all of his money, and has nothing left for the fee. Mahesh's father told them that he had some money for him. And, some of Mahesh's cousins and Master said that they would also help him, if he really wanted to register for the course. Within one weeks' time, Mahesh registered for the Practical bookkeeping course at Hemingway's Correspondence School.

Mahesh studied very hard to get the certificate of practical bookkeeping. It was not very easy for him, since he worked seven days in the poultry farm, playing soccer, and helping his uncle and mom on their farm.

Mahesh's uncle and his father needed everyone working on the farm every weekend. Including Mahesh's brother who was in college. As well as his cousin Bro, who just got married, and worked in Suva City. His mom and sister who did not attend any school, had to be on the farm every day.

Mahesh's schedule was very tight. He would get up early every morning for soccer practice, and then go to the poultry farm for a full day. Then practice again after work, then studied. He wanted to quit his full time job. His father was not happy about this and got mad. So Mahesh decided not to quit the job, but started studying while on the poultry farm. When Mahesh got a little time, he would read the books.

Around this time Mahesh and Master got selected to play soccer for the district team. Now there was a problem again. Practices were okay, but they had to stay at the camp for more practices. Luckily, the manager of the soccer team allowed them to stay off camp, and come for practices every day. When Mahesh had to go to the tournament for the weekend, his father took care of the poultry farm for him. His father helped him because he didn't want someone else to learn about this job, but Mahesh was not much worried now, because he was thinking about moving out of this small town.

After the soccer tournament, Mahesh had his exam. And Mahesh did not pass the exam. He told Master that this was not for him and he could not do this. His cousin replied, "Do you know what 'Chupat' and 'Bahilla' means? Chupat means stupid and bahilla means people with no value and no future. They have no manners. And do you know why your father put you in the poultry farm to clean the birds poop? It is for you to get some lesson. Did you know that he also gave some money for your fees?" After hearing this, Mahesh started studying very hard again so that he can pass the exam this time. With his cousin's help he did pass the exam, and now he has a diploma in practical bookkeeping.

Stick Fighting Story

One day, Mahesh and his cousin were playing with a stick about 1" thick. They were playing around fighting, with the adults nearby. While they were playing, an old man came up to them and said, "Oh, so you guys know how to fight with sticks?" Mahesh did not know him, but he knew his father and uncle knew him. The old man told Mahesh as well as everyone else that he was a good fighter back in his time. To prove it, he told Mahesh to hit him with the stick. Mahesh's father told Mahesh not to do it, and to go back to playing, but the old man kept taunting Mahesh to hit him with the stick. Mahesh's father kept stopping him from trying, because he knew the old man would try and grab Mahesh's leg and throw him before Mahesh could strike him with the stick. The old man kept saying to come, come and hit him. One of Mahesh's cousins, told the old man that Mahesh did not know how to fight with the stick, he wanted the old man to keep egging Mahesh on, and because he knew, Mahesh would hit him hard. His cousin worked on the farm with Mahesh and knew him very well. His cousin was a big troublemaker, and wanted Mahesh to hit this man.

The old man was running around Mahesh and insisted that Mahesh try and hit him. He kept watching Mahesh's legs and hands movements. Mahesh looked to his uncle, he got his signal to do it. Mahesh lifted his stick up and turned sideways and hit the old man very hard. The old man was on the ground before he could reach Mahesh's legs.

While on the ground, the old man says "Oh yes, this boy knows how to play with sticks." Mahesh's father got mad at Mahesh and told him to get lost and tell one of his older cousins to take the old man to the hospital. Mahesh's eldest cousin took him to the hospital to make sure he was okay. The doctor gave him some painkillers and ice cubes. He was fine.

Carrom Board Story

Mahesh, his cousin and his friends would usually play carrom board on Friday nights, at his second cousin's house. Everyone would give money to purchase liquor. The 80 proof rum was the cheapest drink that you could buy those days. Mahesh's second cousin's house was about 2 miles from Mahesh's place. Mahesh and his cousin, Master, had to walk down to this house in the dark. There were no lights on the road. They were not afraid of being robbed, but they were afraid of the dogs. They knew which house had dangerous dogs. Mahesh and his cousin had to run and throw stones if the dogs came after them. Sometimes Mahesh and his cousin took a bike. They had only one bike and Mahesh and Master would always have to ride the bike together.

Mahesh hanging out with friends and family in Tailevu.

Fishing for a Big Fish

One day Mahesh was fishing in the river and caught a small fish about six inches long. He looked at the fish for a long time and threw the fish back. His two cousins and some friends from the neighbourhood were watching him. One of them asked Mahesh why he looked at the fish for so long and threw it back. Was this fish poisonous? Mahesh told them the fish was not poisonous but it was not the fish he was looking for. He needed a big fish. Mahesh told them that he wanted a big fish. Big meaning really big, bigger than himself. Mahesh told them they will never understand. To catch this kind of fish, he has to get out of Tailevu or even out of Fiji. All of them started laughing at him.

From this day forward Mahesh started dreaming big. Big, big dreams. But, it was not easy to find a job in Tailevu town, because this town was very small and his dreams were very big. To achieve his goal he needed to get out of this town. Every day he read the newspaper to see if there were any job openings. Those days they did not have phones in their house. He had to send his resume. It was not easy to find a job through a resume because sending the application through mail would take two to three days.

Luluvia Island

Mahesh survived many times. One instance was when he went deep-sea fishing with Master, and his two best friends. One of his friends (and second cousin) was a fisherman. When they were in the middle of the deep sea the weather changed suddenly. There was heavy wind and rain. The fisherman was driving the boat, Mahesh's duty was to hold the benzine light. There were big waves and the water was coming in the boat. His cousin and his friend had to throw the water back in the sea. Everyone was busy, no one talked to each other. The fisherman told everyone that he couldn't turn the boat back because of very heavy wind and the giant waves. It could cause the boat to tip over and they would all die. They had to keep going forward until they reached an island call Luluvia. He was pretty sure would be able to reach the island, and if not, then only God could save them. Since it was dark, they could not see anything. The fisherman was also not sure if the island was in front of them or not, but he did not say anything because he didn't want to scare anyone.

Everyone was scared but no one became upset. They kept doing what they had to do. The boat moved very slowly against the big waves. After some time the wind cut down and the fisherman laughed and thanked God they survived. The Island was right in front of them. After about one hour they reached the island. This fisherman was very knowledgeable, he knew by the sound of the wind, which direction to go to reach the island. Luckily, someone had built a shed with coconut leaves on the island. They all went in the shed and sat close to each other in the middle of the shed, holding each other to keep warm. They were hungry but the food was in the boat, but because of snakes and they were scared the heavy wind would cause coconuts to fall on them; no one wanted to go back in the boat. One of them had some food, but they didn't have water to drink. As soon as they started eating, they attracted snakes because of the smell of the food and the light. They became very quiet, no one talked or moved.

The fisherman wanted to smoke. He asked Mahesh to grab the cigarettes. The cigarette packet was close to Mahesh and one of the snakes was next to the packet. When Mahesh quickly grabbed the packet, he burned his hand in the benzine light. His friend tied a red cloth as a bandage, which made it more attractive to the snake. He still has that scar on his right hand. Next morning, they started getting worried about playing soccer. They decided to go back even if the weather did not calm down. They had soccer every Sunday and this time their team was playing against a very strong team. This was a very important game for them because it was selection week and they were all the best players on their team. The weather was not quite settled but they took another risk, however this time they went during the day. Riding towards the waves was not as dangerous. They arrived home safely for their soccer game.

Hurricane Sport Club

S occer was more important for them than their life. These guys were crazy for soccer and also for the selection for the inter-district tournament. Mahesh, his cousin Master and second cousin had been selected for inter-district tournament along with two other players from his team.

The Fiji Indian Football Association was founded in year 1938, and they changed the name from Fiji Indian Football Association to Fiji Football Association in year 1962. In 1964, for the first time, inter-district tournament was held in Suva City. Mahesh was only seventeen years old at that time. The players were paid three dollars per day for three days plus tickets for all three-day games, breakfast and dinner. They had to provide their own lunch. All the players had to stay in the school, the dinner was provided if you stayed in the school at dinner time, because the food was cooked in the school.

Those days there was no pool system. Once your team lost the game, the team was out of the tournament and you were free to go on your own. They thought their team would lose the first game, so Mahesh and his cousins made plans to go to their relative's house for dinner and drinks. Somehow, their team won the first game, but their plan was fully organized, so they decided to sneak from the school, and go to their relatives' house for dinner and drinks. They were drinking and dancing till 2am. Next morning when they came back, all of them were sweating. When their manager asked where they had been, Mahesh quickly replied they were warming up, practicing on the ground. The manager was pleased and told them get ready for their next game at 11am. It was a very hot day and they did not have any energy left in their body but they all played. Their team lost the game by ten goals. His second cousin was the goal keeper and he missed all the easy balls. When the manager asked his cousin, he replied there must have been something in the food that they ate this morning.

After one week, the management of Tailevu district football association found out about the incident. The management suspended the whole team from participating in Tailevu district football competition for one year. The management did not suspend the players, they suspended the team. Their team's name was Hurricane Sport Club. Some of the team players were very upset. They wanted to play and went on to join other teams. The players did not complain to Master because he was the team manager and he taught in the same school. He was well respected. So after two weeks, everyone went to Mahesh and complained that it was not their fault and they will join some other team. Mahesh spoke to his cousin and his cousin registered a new team under a new name. This time the name was Diamond Sport club with the same players but different uniform and he paid all the money for registration and other fees. After one year they changed the name again back to Hurricane Sport Club.

Random Jobs

Mahesh's uncle started a timber business on trial. Mahesh went with them in the jungle to help them. When his uncle and cousins were taking a lunch break, Mahesh took a chainsaw to cut down a tree. As soon as he started the chainsaw and touched the tree, the chainsaw bounced back. He almost cut himself in half. He quickly put the chainsaw away and did not tell anyone about this incident because he wanted to go with them again. It was fun for him to play in the jungle. The most fun was when they bought the timber logs through the river. Those days they did not have heavy machines. They used a pair of bulls and floated the timber logs in the river for transportation. Mahesh also liked to hunt. He was fast in the jungle. If he saw a goat, he would go for it. His family liked goat meat. They are Hindu, but they ate goat meat, chicken and fish but not beef. The timber business did not last long because it was time consuming and very risky if you did not have proper machinery or equipment.

One time there was an opening for young farmers to go to New Zealand to learn about dairy farming. It was the New Zealand government's scheme to help Fiji farmers to get better knowledge in dairy farming. They needed only three young farmers from the Tailevu district, for three years to work with New Zealand farmers with very little pay. Mahesh also applied for the position. He was interviewed a couple of times but was not selected because he was very skinny. Mahesh was so upset but he never relinquished his dreams about his future.

Farming and Cousin Stories

Mahesh's cousins were like friends. One of his cousins, Raven, was always getting into trouble. If anything went wrong in the village, he was the first one to be blamed. One night Raven asked Mahesh to come with him. Mahesh knew his cousin might be up to no good, asked him where they were going. His cousin just told Mahesh to follow him. They stopped in front of one of their neighbour's house, not very far from his own. When Mahesh asked him what they were doing there, his cousin replied that he met the neighbour's daughter in town and she was giving him looks. Raven believed she wanted to say something to him, but could not because her mom was with her. Mahesh asked Raven if this girl knew that he was coming tonight. He replied no. Mahesh told him to try going to the back of the house. Those days there wasn't any electricity in Tailevu. The girl's father had a benzine light hanging near the front door. Her father and one of his friends were drinking beer in the veranda. Mahesh was told to stay put, and be a lookout to warn Raven if he sees someone coming. His cousin crawled behind the hibiscus plant towards the back of the house. As soon as he passed half way, the girl's father came out to where his cousin was hiding.

Raven could not move because the girl's father would have seen him. Mahesh thought his cousin was caught, since the father was standing right in front of him. He was so worried, but could not say anything, or Raven would be caught. A few seconds later, Mahesh saw exactly what the father was up to. It looks like he just finished his 6 pack of beer and needed a place to relieve himself.

The father ended up peeing all six beers on Raven. His cousin took the whole six pack of beer on him. He had to just take it without making a sound. Mahesh could only watch and laugh and laugh. He had to push his cousin into the river to rinse himself off.

Another day, Raven and his father were padding rice. Mahesh was going to help them. His cousin knew that Mahesh was coming over, and knew that he would sit or lay in the shady spot under a tree. As Mahesh walked to the padding area, Raven placed some cow dung on the shady spot and hid it with dry grass, so it was not visible. Before Mahesh reached the spot, his uncle told him to chase a calf away from eating the rice plant. While Mahesh was doing this, his uncle went to sit in that same spot under the tree. Raven tried to stop his father but he was too late. Mahesh's uncle became furious and went to change his pants. He told Mahesh, "this was your cousin's plan for you, but I ended up sitting in the cow dung".

Mahesh could not stop laughing. Mahesh cleaned up the spot and put some more hay on top. Then he sat right in the same spot because that was the only shady spot.

Another time, Raven was padding rice, when one of the bulls looked like it wanted to make a "drop". Usually when the bull wants to drop, they lift their tail. Then the bull is pulled out of the padding area, and they would put some hay on it and collect it afterwards, and throw it outside. Raven wanted to catch the dung with both hands, using hay so his hands would not get dirty. Then his plan was to throw it on Mahesh. As soon as saw the bull was about to drop and lifted his tail, Raven stopped it and took some hay in his hands and got ready to catch the dung. However, right before dropping, the bull coughed hard. And, all the dung flew on Raven's face. He called Mahesh for help and asked for some water to clean his eyes. Mahesh couldn't stop laughing and took him to the river. When Raven was about to dive in, his father came and asked Mahesh what happened. Mahesh explained exactly what happened.

First Big Job

Mahesh was very upset for not getting a job in the big city, even though he had a Diploma in Practical Bookkeeping. Mahesh was sending applications to every job opening he would see in the newspaper. One day he sent his resume to Mr. Tom Edward asking if he needed assistance in his office. Mr. Edward showed the letter to Mahesh's father. Mahesh's father became very frustrated and went home to ask Mahesh why he wrote this letter to Mr. Edward. Good thing Mahesh was with his cousin Master, he explained to Mahesh's dad that there was nothing wrong with this. Mahesh just asked for a job. Mr. Edward should reply or call Mahesh and say he did not need anyone to help in the office. True to Master's word, that is what exactly happened. Mr. Edward called Mahesh and said I did not have much to do in my office, but I will try to find something in Suva City for you the next time I go to the Bank. Every Thursday, Mr. Edward would go to Suva City bank for money to pay all his workers. Mahesh felt so happy, and told his father that Mr.

Edward would find employment for him in Suva City. Maybe even in the bank.

One day, his cousin from Suva City, came to Tailevu with his manager. His manager went to Tailevu very often because he got married to someone that lived on the same street as one of Mahesh's second cousins. Mahesh was talking to him and showed him his diploma. Mahesh bought a bottle of rum as a gift, and asked him if he had any job openings, please let him know. Mahesh said to the manager that he would be available at any time and no matter how much the pay, he will be glad to accept it. And, within one month's time, his cousin came to him and said that he had some good news. Mahesh's cousin told him that we are giving him a chance to work in their store.

Mahesh's cousin told Mahesh that he was promoted to assistant manager, and would be his manager. Mahesh's cousin told him that he could have this job under one condition, Mahesh would have to work hard, and do everything that he was told to do. He said that he would have to work under a lot of pressure, because it is a very busy shop. Mahesh would also have to clean and place materials on the shelves. Mahesh was so happy and said to his cousin, "No problem." and that he has a lot of experience cleaning. Mahesh asked his cousin "You're not kidding, right?" His cousin replied "Not this time. Get ready, you will be going with me on Monday." Mahesh was so happy he told everyone about the job in Suva City. This was a very big deal for him, he got a job in a big city. He went to his sister-in-law, and told her there will be no more cleaning Tom's eggs.

Mahesh loved the idea of working in Suva. It is the political, economic, cultural center of Fiji. A lot of major companies had their regional headquarters located in Suva.

The company Mahesh joined was called Industrial Marine Engineering Limited, (IMEL) a wholly-owned subsidary of the Carpenter Group. It was one of the largest and best equipped engineering works in the south pacific. In Fiji this store was situated alongside Walu Bay in Suva City.

On the first day on his new job, Mahesh was excited as well as scared. He did not know what he had to do. First thing in the morning, he was told to clean and sweep the floor, which he didn't mind doing. It was much better than the poultry farm. Everything was going really well. After one week, the pressure started to build when he was told to find out about the stock on the shelves. Product knowledge was hard, there were so many materials on the shelves, and so many types of nails. Mahesh has never seen this many types of nails in his life. And some nails had different names, like bronze nail, some customers asked for boat nails, and some customers would say anchor fast nail. These were all the same nails.

There were so many types of nuts and bolts with different types of thread. This kind of store was not found in small towns. He was totally lost. The manager and his cousin did not like customers waiting for a long time at the counter. His other colleagues gave him a hard time as well. They would pass all the orders to him that requires hard work, like cutting brass and copper rods, filling nails in the bags, and pulling and cutting thick steel wire ropes. Most of the time Mahesh had to do these kinds of jobs, while his colleagues just made invoices. Mahesh did not mind doing this kind of hard work, but this was not his dream for the future. He did not want to go back to the poultry farm either. Sometimes he would go to the back of the store and cry. However, he knew he did not want to go back to Tailevu for sure, so he kept doing it for six more months.

Then one day, Mahesh went to his cousin who was the assistant manager, and asked him if he had to do this type of work all the time. His cousin told Mahesh, that he had to improve his English and learn the names of every product on the shelves. He said to Mahesh, "Your pronunciation was not that good, is your denture not fitting properly?" Mahesh just walked away but his cousin called him back. His cousin advised Mahesh, to do this right he would have to go to school part time, and complete a stores and stock control course. The institute was not very far, just one bus from there.

Mahesh could not refuse his cousin and decided to take the course. He asked one of his colleagues to join him. The colleague agreed and they both registered in the college. The course was only for six months.

The store where Mahesh was working was one mile from the head office, inside the timber yard. Every time they needed any stationary or supplies from the head office, Mahesh had to walk down to get it. One day as soon as he came back, they sent him back to the head office again for some more supplies. It was a very hot day, so the manager told him that he can take the company transport, but first he would have to show the manager his driver's licence. Now, more than ever, Mahesh wanted his driver's licence very badly.

Learning to Drive Story

Before Mahesh went to Suva City, he was driving his brother-in-law's car, but only on the farm grounds. He had a driver's licence for tractors, and a learner's permit to drive light vehicles, but his brother-in-law did not give him the car to drive on the road. Mahesh had a licence to drive a tractor, but it was not as easy to get one for a car, especially since he had no experience driving in a big city. Mahesh wanted to be a good driver, so he took lessons from an instructor. One of his colleagues helped him find a good instructor and sometimes his cousin would give him lessons in his car. In Fiji, only standard transmission cars were available in those days. During the driving test, the examiner asked him to stop on a hill, and move without rolling back. If the car rolled back even an inch, the examiner would not give him the licence.

After failing a few times, Mahesh finally passed and got his driver's licence. Mahesh was so happy he got the licence, because now he would not have to walk down to bring supplies.

Boxing at Work

As time passed, Mahesh gained some experience driving the car, and was able to learn how to do sales and stock control in the store. During lunch time some of his colleagues would go in the back of the store and practice boxing. Mostly those who worked in the warehouse. Mahesh had an hour lunch break, so he would join them and eventually became friends with them. Mahesh had some boxing experience from home. When he boxed with them, he realized how strong he was, because of his hard labour work in the farm from chopping wood, biking and horse riding. He became lean, strong and fast. Mahesh was good at boxing, and everyone started to like him.

In the warehouse, one of his colleagues was a professional boxer. He did not box in the warehouse, but sometimes would coach them. One day he went to Mahesh's cousin, the assistant manager, and ask if Mahesh could join his club, but Mahesh's cousin answered "No".

Thank You God!

After one year at this job, inventory time came again. And again, Mahesh had to do all of the cleaning and counting nuts and bolts. Plus he would have to keep all of the items in good order, so that when the inspectors came, everything had to be in good order. Mahesh liked this because there was a lot of overtime and meal money, only sometimes he finished very late.

Mahesh had to walk to a bus stand alone when he worked late, but Mahesh was not afraid of anyone. In Fiji, people did not carry guns, and Mahesh knew if someone came to rob him, he could run fast and fight back. Those days Fijians did not fight anyone who was weaker than them. One day Mahesh was standing at the bus stand, waiting for his bus to arrive. When he saw a drunk man coming from a bar towards him. This man was so drunk, he was stumbling back and forth, and side to side. This man asked for money from anyone that passed him. As soon as he arrived at the bus stand, the man dropped on the platform with his mouth open. He started praying to God 'Please God, give me something to drink', after saying this over and over again, he fell asleep with his mouth open.

After a few minutes, a dog come and raised his leg and give him a drink. The drunk was so happy; he got up and started talking to his God. Saying, "Thank you God. I will pay you back. I will give you some fruit on my payday."

Mahesh was watching him all this time and start laughing loudly, the drunk man turned to him and asked him why he was laughing so loudly. Mahesh pointed to the dog, and said to the drunk man, "There is your God." The drunk became mad at Mahesh and chased him but could not run as fast as Mahesh.

When the inspectors came, Mahesh couldn't believe it, he was his cousin. He was Mahesh's mom's brother's son. This was an easy inventory because the inspector helped him. If there were any mistakes with counting he corrected it and the inspector gave a very good report to the head office. The inspector also mentioned in his report that the new person was a very hard working person and had a lot of knowledge of the products. From this time on, the manager, Mahesh's other cousin who was the assistant Manager, along with all of his colleagues started liking Mahesh very much, and put him in charge of stock and inventory.

Mahesh's Brother Moving Out

Some time passed, Mahesh's brother, Sagan, was hired to be a radiologist at the government hospital. He wanted to move out from his cousin's house to a room he found very close to the hospital. The room was very small and cheap because they had to share the kitchen and toilet with others. The toilet was outside and you had to take your own toilet paper or water with you. Mahesh and his brother moved out from their cousin's house and stayed in one small bedroom. Most of the time Mahesh did all of the cooking because his brother worked late at the hospital, especially on Fridays and weekends. There were a lot of lot accident cases.

Car Accident

After all of his hard work and obtaining his driving licence Mahesh was promoted to be a sales representative. He was given a company car to go out in the city to small job sites and industrial business shops for canvassing. Mahesh was so happy because he liked driving but could not afford to buy his own car. One day he got lucky again. His best friend's brother bought a brand new car and his friend wanted Mahesh to go with him for driving practice on a Sunday morning.

To learn to drive, you need a licensed driver in the car, so Mahesh went with him. Mahesh's friend had no experience driving a car before and Mahesh was a new driver with no experience in teaching. Mahesh's friend started driving and went on a major road that was more than fifty miles per hour. He wanted to overtake a car that was turning right, but ended up hitting the car. Mahesh kept telling him to stop and pointed out that the car was turning right but his friend thought he would be to overtake the car. His friend's brother's new car, just one week old, was a total write-off. People asked who was driving this car, is he alive? And what about the passenger? Is he dead. But they both got out of the wreckage without a scratch. Mahesh survived again.

Hurricane Bibi

In October 1972, there was a big hurricane in Fiji. They named it Hurricane Bibi. Due to heavy rain, there was a big flood in Tailevu, where Mahesh's parents lived. Their house was totally destroyed. This was the biggest hurricane after a long time. Some big companies helped their employees if their house was damaged. Mahesh's company was also giving building material to their employees who were employed for more than one year as a loan. The loan was for five thousand dollars. Mahesh's manager and his cousin decided to help Mahesh. They spoke to one of the builders to draft and estimate the amount of materials needed to build a three-bedroom house on concrete posts, about five feet high. In the meantime, Mahesh and his cousin submitted an application for a loan, which was approved.

They purchased all the building materials; the timber was supplied from their timber yard for a very good price and transported to Tailevu. Mahesh's father and his cousins from Tailevu with some carpenters, started building the house. Now Mahesh had to pay for the loan and give the same amount to his cousin every payday. It was very hard for him to tell his parents that he did not have any money left when they needed money to pay wages to the carpenters. His father also needed to buy some small materials. Mahesh did not have any money left. His father understood, but it was very hard to explain to his mom.

Mahesh's brother helped, but he worked for the government hospital. In the government hospital people did not get good pay in the beginning, but he did send some money when possible. Mahesh's mom thought Mahesh was not helping, only her other son helped to build the house. Mahesh decided to find a second part time job to send some money home. But he did not want to quit playing soccer. He took a loan from a friend, and sent the money home to complete the construction on time. Within three months' time, with hard work and help from everyone in the village, a nice house was built on posts. This time there was no risk from floods and hurricanes. They used all hardwood timber and made it hurricane proof. The house had wooden floor. Mahesh's mom did not have to level the floor every month with mud and cow dung. She was very happy for the first time in her married life. She had her own house with wooden floor and no leaky roof, built on their farmland. Mahesh believed that if he did not move to the city, they wouldn't have had such a nice family home.

Dislocated Knee

Mahesh had been playing soccer for the big city club, but it was hard to be selected for the inter-district tournament. Mahesh was not selected for practice in this big city team, so he decided to go every weekend to Tailevu to play for their district team. Mahesh could be selected for Tailevu team if he came every week for the practice. Finally, he was selected to practice in Tailevu to play in the inter-district tournament. Also, the management and the official of the Tailevu District team liked him very much. They made him the team captain because he practiced in the big city club and had improved his soccer skills. In the tournament, his team drew to play one of the strongest teams. It was a very hot day at 10am and his team lost the game. Those days once the team lost the game, they were out of the tournament and his team was out of tournament on the first day.

The team manager and officials were very upset and suspended Mahesh from the team. Now he could only play for small businesses and religious teams. There was a soccer tournament for businesses in Suva City. Mahesh played for his company's soccer team. While he was playing, his right knee got dislocated. The officials took him to the hospital for treatment. The X- Ray showed no signs of any broken bones, but when he walked his right knee moved to the side. Mahesh knew someone who could set the knee in the right position. Mahesh was taken to him by his friend. As soon as this person saw Mahesh, he knew it was from soccer and told Mahesh to keep quiet for a moment. Then that man smiled at him and told him not to worry. He will set his knee, but Mahesh cannot play soccer anymore. The man warned Mahesh that if he played soccer and dislocated his knee again, to not come back to him.

The man asked Mahesh to walk forward towards him without holding anything. When Mahesh walked to him he looked at Mahesh's knee and asked for a towel. The man tied the towel around Mahesh's right knee then told four people to hold him down. Within a second, Mahesh found himself on the ground. This was the second time Mahesh saw stars in the day time. But the man fixed his knee in the right position. Because Mahesh injured himself during a tournament for his company, Mahesh was given two weeks holiday with full pay.

Industrial Marine Limited

In two years' time, Industrial Marine Engineering Limited extended their business. Mahesh's store was changed to Industrial Supplies Limited and moved into a larger building with more sales people and staff. Mahesh's kept his position as a sales representative. Most of the time Mahesh was very busy doing rush deliveries, purchasing and collecting stationary from the head office.

One of the staff members returned from his vacation in Australia. While there, he learned how to do horse betting. This person taught all the staff how to bet on horses, and they started betting on horses daily. If the race was during the day, anyone who wanted to place a bet, gave Mahesh money and the name of the horses they wanted to bet on. Mahesh would place bets for everyone and became too busy doing things not related to sales.

In Suva City, there is a festival known as the Fiji Hibiscus Festival. One of the managers from another department was a part of the Fiji Hibiscus Festival Organization. She wanted Mahesh and one of his colleagues to become a member. She took them to the meeting and they were elected as committee members for five years. The Hibiscus Festival had grown into a nine-day event, drawing large crowds from Viti Levu. The festival was held once a year in August to coincide with the school break. Mahesh and his colleague worked in this charitable organization for one month without pay. Sometimes it was fun for them, because they did not have to pay to attend any events. Mahesh and his colleague's families got free rides. Their major duty was to take care of ground activities.

During the festival week they took a holiday for one week because they had to be on the ground all the time till midnight. Mahesh gave the groundwork contract to a construction company that was owned by one of Mahesh's relatives. His quote was very low compared to other construction companies. Mahesh advised his relatives to increase his quotation because there was a lot of work to be done. This was his first time doing this type of job in Suva. Before this his relative only did small construction jobs in small towns.

The owner of the construction company was very happy with Mahesh and paid Mahesh and his colleague to fix some small things if his labourers were not on site. Mahesh and his colleagues were very happy to work for this charitable organization.

All of the staff was busy doing other things instead of business. After a few years, the Industrial Supplies department's sales started going down. They were not meeting their targets and Mahesh got all of the blame. Mahesh's manager called him in his office and they had a long conversation regarding sales. Mahesh explained to him why he did not get enough time to do canvassing. His manager told him that his first duty was to consider sales and if he did not have time to do a delivery then don't do it. Mahesh's manager told Mahesh that he had to answer to the general manager in the general meeting.

In the general meeting, Mahesh's manager blamed Mahesh for the declining sales. He took all the proof of what Mahesh was doing before and compared it to what he is doing now. His performance had dropped by 80%. He took all of the documents and submitted them to his general manager. Mahesh decided not to do any betting during business hours and no more delivery for the sales staff. Some of the staff complained to the manager that their customers were not happy, because they did not get their supplies on time. The manager told them, it is up to Mahesh, if he has time to do the delivery. Mahesh thought it would be better that the general manager knew Mahesh as a hard working person.

The Industrial Supplies Department was getting out of control. Mahesh's dream was getting nowhere. Mahesh was so worried, he did not want to go back to Tailevu. And his cousin, the assistant manager, also quit the job and migrated to Canada. To a city called Edmonton, Alberta. Mahesh was very upset and didn't know what to do. When he spoke to his colleagues about his dreams and goals, they all laughed at him and started making fun of him.

Mahesh was losing respect for this company. One day he met his best client who was also like his best friend. He was preparing to start a new import and export business, with two partners from Australia. They had rented the office space downtown and hired one office staff member. Mahesh's friend was also one of the directors in this business. They offered Mahesh employment as a sales representative with double the pay of what he was getting from Industrial Marine Engineering Limited. Mahesh accepted the offer, took two weeks' vacation from his job, and mailed the resignation letter to his manager after the vacation. When Mahesh started his new job, he did not have much to do, because they were still organizing everything. Mahesh felt very happy again, he felt like his dream was coming true.

After a few months, Mahesh found out there was not much happening in the office. When he inquired about this, he was told that one of the business partners did not want to proceed with the business anymore. Mahesh's friend had spent a lot of money to bring this business to this level. And went to Australia to find out why his partner did not want to continue. There was no one in the office to speak to, then one day Mahesh saw a big lock hanging on the door. He became very worried and sad. He did not know what to do and whom to talk to. Mahesh went to the receptionist's residence to find out what was happening.

She also had no idea. She thought Mahesh might know. Both Mahesh and the receptionist did not get paid for more than one month. Mahesh did not have any money and his dream was falling apart again. One thing that remained the same, he did not want to go back to his hometown Tailevu again. His father wanted him to come back, giving him all kinds of advice. Mahesh's father told him that he did not have to work on the farm, he can own a business, like driving a taxi or his own passenger van. Mahesh's dream was not to go back, but to move forward. He wanted to move overseas, anywhere, Australia, New Zealand, America or Canada. If Mahesh went back to Tailevu it would not be possible to achieve his dream.

Mahesh had become very sad and mad. He started looking for any type of job in the city. One day Mahesh met one of his former clients. He was a purchasing officer for the government marine department. Mahesh told him what had happened. He also told him that his brother was posted to Labasa hospital. Labasa is a city on another major island of Fiji. Fiji has two main islands call Viti Levu, and Vanua Levu. (Viti Levu's capital city is Suva, and Vanua Levu's is Labasa.) Since Sagan had to move, Mahesh was left to pay the rent and all expenses on his own. This client went and spoke to Mahesh's old manager, as they were good friends. He insisted that the manager call Mahesh back. He told him that Mahesh is a very quiet and nice person. He has always been dedicated to his clients. This person also mentioned to Mahesh's manager that he has a girl in his family, and has a plan to arrange a marriage between them. Mahesh's old manager agreed to call him back. One day Mahesh's old manager called him, and told him that he had found out from one of his clients, that he was not employed. Mahesh told him everything that was happening in his life. And after some discussion he had been hired again, same position as before - a sales representative, with the same pay he was getting when he left Industrial Supplies Limited.

After one year's time, Mahesh's client, the one who requested his manager for his employment, came and asked Mahesh's manager about the marriage between Mahesh and his sister. Mahesh's manager mentioned this to him. Mahesh could not directly refuse him, because this client helped him get this job back. Mahesh told his manager about his dream, and if he gets married to this family, all of his dreams and future would be done. Mahesh told his manager if he can marry someone from overseas, there would be a chance to migrate, but his manager just shook his head. Then Mahesh asked his manager, what would be the best thing to do. His manager told Mahesh to visit the relative's residence this weekend but not commit to anything. They went to the client's relative's house but did not make any commitment. Mahesh's father also wanted him to get married, but Mahesh wanted his dream to come true first.

After showing his hard work and commitment to his customers through dedication and relationship building, Mahesh was given the opportunity to take internal sales courses and customer relations training. After the training, management wanted him to do sales for all departments. This company had six different departments in the same location, such as boat building, electrical, foundry, steel and an engineering department. Mahesh had to move to the marketing department to learn about the materials for all the departments and he worked very hard to build product knowledge for each department. By helping all of these departments, all of the department managers started to like him. In a very short time, he became a very successful sales assistant for all departments. With his new training, he was very good with dealing with customers, so he was transferred to the marketing department. In the marketing department there wasn't much to do. Most of the time he had to collect blueprints from the builders and pass it on to the appraisal department for a quote. Once the appraisal was complete, he had to draft the quotation letter and submit it back to the builders. This was needed to be done very quickly before the tender expired.

Mahesh had been doing this for a couple years, and figured out that most of the builders were just using this company to work for them. Mahesh's superiors had been doing this for a long time and used company's money to entertain the builders' staff. When Mahesh mentioned this to the appraisal department manager, the manager replied he knew and told Mahesh to talk to his own manager. His seniors had been doing this for a long time, and they were very busy all of the time. One day Mahesh was in the office by himself and he got a call from one of the builders to come and get a drawing for an electrical quote. They told Mahesh to come quickly because it was a rush order as the tender was closing that afternoon.

Mahesh told them he was alone in the office and couldn't come rightway. He would be able to come as soon as he gets time. They were very upset with him. They called Mahesh's manager and the senior salesman. This senior salesperson always rushed to collect the drawings and would give some kind of gift to the builders as well. When they found out that Mahesh did not come and collect the drawing, one of the builder's estimators and Mahesh's manager called the electrical department manager. They complained that Mahesh was not taking this job seriously. The electrical department manager spoke to Mahesh. Mahesh told them that the builders had called him, but he did not take them seriously after he found out that the builders have not given their company any orders for a long time, even when they won the tender. They would shop round again for a better quote with smaller companies and would give the order to them. They were just using Mahesh's company for a quote. The electrical department manager totally agreed with Mahesh.

The next day, the senior salesman came up to Mahesh and shouted at him. He told Mahesh to come to the manager's office right away and that this may be his last day in the company. As he was shouting, the general manager and appraisal department's manager all came to the marketing department manager's office. The senior salesman shouted at Mahesh again for not collecting the drawing, and blamed

Mahesh for the builders getting mad at the company. Mahesh explained to all the managers that he had been investigating for a long time and found out that these builders were just using the company's services. Our company has not seen any orders from these builders, even if the builders got the tender. The general manager asked if this was true but before the marketing manager could reply Mahesh replied to him. He told the General Manager that the marketing manager asked Mahesh to investigate this matter and they were going to make arrangements with the builders. If the builders got the tender then their company should get the order. The general manager was impressed with Mahesh and the marketing manager was happy with Mahesh as well for protecting him. The senior salesman was very upset because he was doing this for a long time and all of the builder's estimators were his best friends. The senior salesman became frustrated, he was using the company's money to entertain all of the builder's estimators. From then on, the marketing manager cut the senior salesman's allowance.

Ever since that meeting, Mahesh took over most of the senior salesman's jobs, because of the new arrangement made with the builders. Most of the builders agreed and the company started getting some orders from all builders. All the managers were very happy with Mahesh because their target got easier to complete. Every month, Mahesh's manager allowed him to go around the Island for canvassing on company expense. Before this was only done by the senior salesman.

It's not that Mahesh wasn't always nice to everyone. Yes, he was very energetic and a strong person. All of his life he worked hard on the farm, feeding chickens, running around in the bush and he also worked for Mr. Tom Edward. Mahesh had to fill water from the well for cows to drink, for more than four hundred cows. Mahesh did not get to rest, no one else wanted to do this kind of job. After doing all of this, he also played soccer. Mahesh liked being involved in all outside activities. Mahesh liked swimming. Those days it was easy to start fights on the soccer field, Mahesh was never scared to get involved and also he practiced boxing with his cousins, so his hand was fast and quick. If anyone wanted to slap or hit his head, even for fun, his hand quickly protected him automatically. Mahesh also went to one private small group to learn karate.

Mahesh was newly transferred to the marketing department and his office was having a Christmas party. Usually, the marketing department did all of the arrangements for these types of events. Mahesh's duty was to serve beer to everyone. They did not have a fridge at that time. They had to fill a cooler with beer and top it with ice cubes. Sometimes the beer didn't get cold because of the hot weather. During the Christmas season it is extremely hot in Fiji. Mahesh gave someone a beer, that wasn't very cold. That person threw the beer in Mahesh's face. Next thing you know, that person was on the floor. Everyone became very quiet. Mahesh just walked out of the office and went home. After two days, when he went back to the office, no one spoke about the incident. Mahesh asked his manager what happened after he left. His manager told him to just forget about it, and asked Mahesh if he knew who that person was. Mahesh replied no, that he never seen him before. His manager told Mahesh that it was the new manager for the electrical department. The general manager told that person it was his fault for throwing beer in Mahesh's face.

One time, Mahesh was invited to a Christmas party at the Grand Pacific Hotel. The Grand Pacific Hotel was one of the most famous and expensive hotels in Suva. After drinking a few glasses of alcohol, Mahesh asked a girl for a dance. Mahesh knew this girl for a long time, but she refused, and told Mahesh that she was not feeling well. Mahesh walked away. A few minutes later, he saw this same girl dancing with someone else. She would come in front of Mahesh and shake her butt. After doing this a couple of times, Mahesh stood up and kicked her on her backside, knocking her over.

Moments later, Mahesh found himself outside of hotel on the ground. When his friend came and asked what had happened, Mahesh started to laugh and told his friend the security officer threw him out. Mahesh asked his friend to bring him a drink. His friend went inside, grabbed two glasses of alcohol and they drank outside, sitting on the grass. Eventually, two cops came and told them to go home before they put them in jail. Those days people knew soccer players very well. Luckily, Mahesh's friend was a very famous soccer player. He played for the Suva team and had been selected to play for Fiji's team in the south pacific tournament. These two cops knew them very well.

Getting Married

Mahesh's luck was about to turn around. There was a Fijian family that was immigrating to Canada very soon, and were looking to get one of the sisters married before they all leave, as this sister was not going with them. Only a few brothers as well as the parents were going to leave to Canada. They had another brother that was already in Canada, and before the family split up more, the parents wanted to witness this daughter getting married.

One of the brothers was the owner of a trucking company that worked with the timber yard that Mahesh worked at. He was speaking to the timber yard manager, who was previously the Industrial Supplies department manager. As they were talking, he mentioned their situation, and how they wanted to get his sister married right away, as they were leaving the country very soon. The brother told the timber yard manager that they would help whoever married their sister, migrate to Canada. The manager told him that he thinks he knows someone, and will get back to him soon.

The manager went to another timber yard manager, and then this manager went to talk to Mahesh. This manager just went up to Mahesh and said, "Looks like your dreams are about to come true." He told him about the family, and they actually happened to be one that Mahesh knew very well. He explained the whole situation, and that they have a sister who they wanted to get married before they leave for Canada. Mahesh agreed to meet with the family.

Therefore, this manager made arrangements with the girl's family to meet Mahesh's family. A few weeks later, some of the girl's family members and the manager went to Mahesh's father's house in Tailevu to talk about the marriage, but the girl did not come with them. After a long conversation, both families agreed to proceed with the marriage in the near future. Once everything was confirmed, Mahesh's future father-in-law took out two dollars from his pocket and gave them to Mahesh, stating that from that day forward Mahesh is his son. Within a couple months, the girl's family went to see Mahesh's father again, they wanted the wedding ceremony to take place within a month. They told Mahesh's father that they were in a rush because they were emigrating to Canada very soon.

Mahesh's father called Mahesh to come home, explaining that they needed to talk about his wedding. His father told him that his future father in-law is at the house, and he wants Mahesh to get married within one month. Mahesh didn't believe them, he thought they just wanted to rush the wedding thinking that Mahesh might change his mind. Mahesh's father said what if they are speaking the truth? And if they emigrate to Canada, they could sponsor him. Mahesh told his father that he does not have enough money to get married right now, and asked his father to tell them to wait a little longer. Mahesh's father assured him that they were all going to help him out.

Everyone in the family helped as much as they could. Mahesh's father and mother did all of the shopping for the wedding. They bought the wedding ring, it cost only $1, and a beautiful saree for his bride, it the cheapest they could find in their hometown but was still very nice. His cousins and brothers helped out by doing the grocery shopping. Mahesh's best cousin, Master, also gave some money to his father. Mahesh's job was to arrange the pundit (priest) to conduct the ceremony. One of his friends who was a pundit, so he hoped that he would come and do the wedding ceremony. The pundit Mahesh arranged could not make it on the wedding date because he was busy doing another wedding somewhere else. The pundit sent his son instead, and prepared all of the documents for him.

The weather was very hot on the wedding day. As everyone arrived at the bride's house, the pundit was shaking hands with people while standing outside in the sun. When all of a sudden, a gust of wind sent all of his documents flying in the air. Some of the kids helped the pundit collect the papers, but since the documents weren't numbered, the order was all mixed up. The pundit started reading them all wrong. Mahesh's uncle got mad and asked who arranged this pundit. One of Mahesh's cousins stated that Mahesh arranged it himself. Mahesh's uncle replied that he must have found the cheapest one. Luckily there was another pundit in attendance from the bride's side. Mahesh's uncle had a lot of respect from the family, so when he asked the other pundit to proceed with the ceremony, he did it without any hesitation. This was the beginning of Mahesh and his new wife, Bijma's, life together.

Mahesh and Bijma getting married

Mahesh's in-laws were very nice people. His wife's parents treated him as their own son. The brothers and sisters were very helpful, but their way of thinking was very different from Mahesh's. They liked to party every weekend. One weekend he was invited to his wife's family's house to stay over. There was a wedding in the neighborhood. Mahesh was invited to the wedding as well. Mahesh went to the wedding and started drinking. Mahesh had a bit too much to drink and became very tipsy. One of his new brother-in-laws let him sleep in one of the bedrooms as no one else was in the house and were all at the wedding.

Since the property was in a rural area, there were mosquito nets all around the house. Because of the netting, Mahesh could not see that there was a cat in the house. Later that night, while he was sleeping, the cat peed in the mosquito net, and it went all over him. When Bijma came inside and saw him, he was in a deep sleep. She woke him up right away because it stank very bad. She told Mahesh to go and have a bath. The bathroom was outside, when he went outside to bathe the dogs came running after him. Mahesh called his wife, asking her to stay with him.

Even after bathing, he still smelled very bad. Mahesh told his wife that he needed to go home, but Mahesh did not have a car at that time. Bijma told him that no one will drive him, because they all are drunk. He would have to keep cleaning himself until the smell went way. Mahesh bathed more than four times that night and still the smell would not go away.

The smell was in his mind for more than one week. Whenever he would eat anything, to him it smelled like cat pee. It was a great experience for Mahesh; his first time at his in-law's house.

Trying to Leave Fiji

Mahesh liked his wife's family. His in-laws were all fun-loving people. But, Mahesh had ambitions to be successful. He had big dreams to achieve, however his wife's family wanted to enjoy life. Bijma came from a big family; she had five brothers and three sisters. Big family. Two of her brothers had moved to Canada already. Her oldest sister migrated to the United States of America. All of these people were willing to help Mahesh and his family move out of Fiji, so Mahesh felt that it would only be a matter of time. Mahesh's wife had a younger sister, who was already married. Her husband was posted to Port Vila on a five-year contract as a manager of a movie theater. Port Vila is a city of an Island called Vanuatu. Mahesh's father-in -law, was right, in a very short time most of his wife's family migrated to Canada.

Now everything was moving smoothly. Mahesh's married life was well managed. Bijma stayed home because she thought they would migrate to Canada very soon. Mahesh was doing well in the marketing department. He was canvassing, every month he went round the island, staying in five star hotels, and at nice resorts. Sometimes he took Bijma with him. When he took his wife with him, he would arrange some orders beforehand. Mahesh just had to collect the confirmation order from the clients, and submit it to his manager in the office when he came back. Since Bijma had a big family, he was invited every weekend to someone's house, if he did not go out of the city on business.

A few years later, there were big changes in his company. The timber yard department moved to Carpenter's Timber Yard, because they were under the Carpenter Group. And, the manager of Industrial Supplies, who was also the manager of the timber yard, emigrated to New Zealand.

While all this was happening, the general manager also changed. Industrial Marine Engineering Limited, got a new General Manager from England to replace him.

The senior salesman was told to go and receive the new General Manager from the airport. The International Airport is on the west side of the Island. The senior salesman went and received the new manager from airport. The next day, the senior salesman and his wife made arrangements with the new general manager to have a picnic in pacific harbour. They spent all day at the beach together, and the senior salesman became the General Manager's biggest informant.

For a while, the General Manager and Senior Salesman would both go out for lunch together, and visited some of Mahesh's large clients for introductions. The trouble started again, and this corrupt salesman started giving Mahesh a hard time. The General Manager would always favour this salesman. However, Mahesh needed this job, and he endured on.

After one year, Mahesh's brother-in-law from Canada sponsored him, but the immigration office of Canada declined the application. However, they indicated that it can be reconsidered in the near future.

Again, Mahesh was getting very upset, but he did not relinquish his dreams. Bijma had more education than Mahesh. She always gave him hope. She asked her other brother to sponsor them one more time.

Bijma also had a sister in the United States of America. She asked her sister to proceed with sponsoring their family for the US as well. His wife's sister had been residing in California for more than five years, so she was able to apply for her family. She then found out that to get a landed residence Visa for America it takes more than five years to process, but there would be a high chance of the application being approved. Therefore, they decided to start the process and wait.

Mahesh's brother, Sagan, was now leaving Fiji as well. He was moving to Australia. Before he left for Australia, he gave his car to Mahesh. Mahesh was so happy, and was very lucky because the car was practically brand new. Mahesh felt relieved a bit since he now has a car, but he still wanted to move out, and not stay in Fiji. Mahesh still had some hope, he figured that after his brother resides in Australia for more than five years, he would be able to sponsor him as well. Mahesh was always thinking about ways that he could move out of Fiji.

Mahesh's "new" car.

As another option, Mahesh contacted his old manager that had left to work in New Zealand. He asked him if he would be able to get a work permit Visa for New Zealand. At this point Mahesh would take any opportunity that would get him out of his current situation.

With all of this on his mind, his sales were going down, and on top of that the senior salesman was giving him a hard time, all he could think was that he wanted to move out of Fiji Island as soon as possible.

The senior salesman was trying hard to get Mahesh laid off, or out of the marketing department. Mahesh was a union member and all of the other managers liked him. He was given an opportunity to move in to the Industrial supplies department, as an assistant manager, with the same salary. Mahesh accepted the offer without hesitation. Mahesh wouldn't have to report to the corrupt salesman any more. And Mahesh had prior experience in this department.

This was working out for Mahesh for a while, however after a few years Mahesh's manager was transferred to a different department with more pay, and better position. Which was good and bad for Mahesh, as he was given the opportunity to manage the department by himself, but he had to report to the marketing department, to the same senior salesman.

Taxi Driver Accident

A round this time, Mahesh ended up getting in some big trouble for something he did not do.

One day, while he was driving his brand new car, a taxi driver rear-ended his car. Luckily, the car did not have much damage, but Mahesh still wanted to call the police to make sure there was a report. However, the taxi driver insisted him to not call the police. The taxi driver told Mahesh that he would pay for the repairs.

Mahesh got his car repaired, and when he went to ask the taxi driver for the repair costs, the taxi driver told him to come next week. So Mahesh went to see him after one week, the taxi driver said to come the following week. Every time Mahesh would ask for money to pay the costs to repair his car, he said the same thing, come next week. And after a few times, the taxi driver started ignoring Mahesh. Mahesh was not afraid of anyone. And this time they got in a big argument, and they both started fighting. Some of the other taxi drivers stopped the fight, Mahesh, got very angry and told the driver that he would pay for this. And that he would be very sorry for this.

Those words would come back to haunt Mahesh. Because a week later some looters hired his taxi to a rural area, and the driver was robbed and killed. Police found the body in his car. The police started questioning Mahesh, because of the fight. The crime branch suspected Mahesh, but there was no proof. They gave Mahesh a hard time until they found the real murderers.

Rewa's Farmers Club

As time went on, Mahesh felt that nothing was getting better for him. He felt that he wasn't where he thought he would be in life, and this upset him very much. His wife saw that he was not feeling good, and that he got frustrated all the time and did not want to talk to anyone. Mahesh's wife mentioned this to one of her brothers-in-law, her sister's husband, about his frustration and sadness. So, his brother-in-law took Mahesh to enroll in the Rewa Farmers Club. Mahesh's brother-in-law was a lifelong member of this Club.

Rewa Club was located in the same district where Mahesh was born. They went to meet the secretary for enrollment. When the secretary, a man around the same age as Mahesh, was interviewing Mahesh, they both started talking about their past. Mahesh told him that his birth place and home; Kasavu Rewa. The secretary stared at Mahesh without saying anything for a moment. They both looked like they may have known each other. Then, Mahesh grabbed the secretary's arm and turned it over to look at his wrist.

Mahesh was shocked. When he saw the scar on his hand, his eyes filled with tears. They both then realized who each other were and hugged. The secretary was Babu, Mahesh's friend from childhood. The same friend whose wrist Mahesh cut when he was a young boy.

Father in Law Funeral

After a few years, Mahesh felt that things were starting to be okay. He had a daughter. And his wife was pregnant with their second child. However, they received bad news that his father in-law passed away in Edmonton, Alberta, Canada. Mahesh's brothers-in-law, and mother-in-law wanted Mahesh and Bijma to attend the funeral in Canada. They were willing to pay the airplane fare and all of the expenses for them to attend the funeral in Canada. It was a tough decision, but Mahesh decided to fly to Canada to support the family during the funeral, but he would have to go on his own as his wife was pregnant and could not fly.

Mahesh did not have a valid passport to travel, and his manager was taking vacation in one week. Mahesh's manager was glad that he had a chance to take a vacation after a long time. So, when Mahesh received the call on Saturday morning that his father-in-law passed away, he went to his manager's residence first thing in the morning and explained everything. Mahesh hesitated to tell his manager that he wanted to go to his father-in-law's funeral in Canada, because his manager was planning on leaving for his holiday in one week, and this was his first vacation after five years. Mahesh was his assistant and they both can't be gone at the same time. Finally, his manager said to Mahesh to go first, because the manager's wife insisted that he go for the funeral.

The manager gave Mahesh five weeks' vacation. Mahesh's manager was a good person. He helped Mahesh get his passport done during the weekend. Mahesh had a passport, but it had expired. Mahesh's manager knew someone who worked for the passport office. Mahesh and his manager went to his house, and luckily, they had an application form at the house. Mahesh completed the form, and then they went to his friend who had a photo studio. They made him open his studio on Sunday so that they can take Mahesh's passport photo. Everything was done over the weekend.

Mahesh got his new passport first thing on Monday morning, and his flight was 9pm that night. He had to collect his passport from the passport office and drive across the island to the airport. Mahesh did all this, and drove to his cousin Master's house, which was only ten minutes away from the airport. As soon as Mahesh reached to his cousin's house, he went straight to the washroom and took a shower. He asked his cousin Master to drive him to the airport, and he made it just in time.

April 1982 was the first time Mahesh went to Canada. His flight was from Fiji to Hawaii, then from Hawaii to Los Angeles, Los Angeles to Vancouver, BC, and then finally to Edmonton, Alberta. Mahesh had never seen snow before in his life, only in the movies. It was very cold when he arrived at the Edmonton airport, however his brother-in-law knew Mahesh would be cold and came with a winter coat, and boots for him. The next day one of his brothers-in-law bought him a suit to wear at the funeral. In Fiji they did not wear suits to funerals in those days.

The funeral ceremony was very sad, but Mahesh was glad that he went to support his in-laws and be a part of the prayers. This was his family too.

After the funeral the weather started to get better. Mahesh went out to do some shopping and see what Canada was all about. Most of the time he went to the West Edmonton Mall. This mall is the largest shopping mall in North America. Mahesh never went to a place like this before.

Most of the time Mahesh found the costs were a little high, but good quality. This was Mahesh's first time in Canada, and although it was for a funeral, and the weather wasn't the best, he loved going there.

New Job

Once Mahesh came back from Canada, there were more changes in his company. Mahesh's manager, the one that was in the marketing department was transferred to another branch with better pay, and more responsibilities. And the corrupt salesman was given the opportunity to take over the Industrial Supplies department. Mahesh had no choice, but to work under the same corrupt salesman.

Mahesh felt depressed, after seeing life overseas in Canada, he had even less interest in staying in Fiji.

By now, Mahesh has had his second child, a baby girl. Everyone in the family was so happy. And with the arrival of his new baby, Mahesh was even more determined to have a better life. The corrupt salesman started giving him a very hard time again. The pressure was out of control. Mahesh needed to find a new job as soon as possible.

Fortunately, Mahesh ran into an old friend, one who had employed him before. This friend explained to Mahesh that he had extended his business in the Timber Saw Mill and is also rice farming. He also develops farmland and sells them to farmers. He needed someone that he could trust to help him. And he knew that Mahesh is a very trustworthy person and would be perfect for this position.

The Farm was approximately 50 miles west of Suva City. His friend insisted that Mahesh come and work for him as a manager. He assured Mahesh that this time everything was under control. Mahesh's friend told him that he is the sole proprietor in this business, and Mahesh would be the sales manager in his business. Mahesh would report directly to him, and even his brothers, and some of his relatives were his employees. And they would be under Mahesh's supervision. The only downside was that he wouldn't be able to match the salary that Mahesh was getting from Industrial Marine Engineering. But he was promised an increase his salary in the future. Mahesh accepted the offer and quit Industrial Marine Engineering Limited.

Moving close to Nausori

Mahesh's budget was very tight because of his pay. It was very difficult for Mahesh to stay in the city, pay rent and drive 50 miles every day to the farm. Bijma decided to move to her brother's house. This house was vacant for a long time, since her brother and his family had moved to Canada. This property was in a rural area, about 10 miles east of Suva City. There was no electric power or landline phone in this area. There was no phone access anywhere in the area. If you needed to call someone you had to go to the post office in a small town called Nausori, about three miles away. The toilet was outside, approximately ten yards away from the house. Even so, they moved into this house because the rent was very cheap.

Since Mahesh was sponsored again by Bijma's brother from Canada, and also from her sister in the US. The documents were being processed, so Mahesh thought that he wouldn't have to stay for long. So, he decided to move in and save some money.

Getting Power

After a short time, Mahesh decided they really needed to get power to this house. So, he arranged with the hydroelectric department to supply electric power to this area.

The road in the area was a feeder road that was maintained by the local people. Every time the road needed maintenance, everyone had to come up with some money to repair the road. The neighbours were having a meeting to figure out ways to collect money to maintain the road. Mahesh also attended the meeting and came up with a suggestion. His brother-in-law was a manager of a movie theater, and he could ask him to help them make money by running a movie in his theater for charity. He was confident that his brother-in-law would help him out, as he was very close to Mahesh. Mahesh would call him Buddy.

Mahesh went to talk to his brother-in-law Buddy, and Buddy agreed to help, under one condition, everyone had to help sell tickets. Everyone liked the idea, and they started selling the movie tickets every weekend. They were going house to house selling tickets in a group. In every group there was a car owner to make it easy for them. Most of them liked to be in Mahesh's group, because when people did not buy the tickets, because they already seen the movie, or had other plans, but still gave money to help them. Mahesh used this money to buy beer, and his group enjoyed drinking in the car while selling tickets. Mahesh's group always came up with more money because many people knew him. When they ran the movie, they had enough money to maintain the road professionally.

Eventually, Mahesh asked Buddy to come and build his own house next to Mahesh's. There was a block beside his house. This block his was given to Mahesh by his father-in-law to build a house for himself. Mahesh's father-in-law just told Mahesh you can build your own house if he wanted to, but there weren't any documents made, because the land was native lease. Mahesh did not have enough money to build his own house, and he didn't want to take a loan, because in Mahesh's mind, he will migrate overseas very soon, the land was vacant. Buddy built his nice little house by getting help from the neighbours. The neighbours liked him because he helped them make money to repair the road.

Mahesh decided to renovate the house he was renting. He built a washroom inside the house, and he arranged with one of his cousins, who is a manager in a telephone company, to have a telephone in their home. In a short time, they had a phone line in their area. As time passed by, everything moved very nicely. Mahesh and his brother-in-law lived together. They had a nice house, washroom in the house, electricity and phone. Mahesh had his two girls and his brother-in-law had two boys. Everyone was so happy, the two sisters were very much attached to each other, and Buddy was a very nice person, him and Mahesh always hung out together.

Watermelon Farming

Mahesh was doing well in his new sales position. He was developing farmland and selling to farmers, this was very easy for him because he is very good in sales and had a background in farming. The only thing that he had to deal with was that Mahesh had a long drive every day, and sometimes he had to drive two times, if the customers wanted to see the farmland.

On the farm, instead of rice farming, Mahesh planted watermelon. This was the first time in Fiji someone produced this kind of watermelon. Mahesh had to find a market overseas, so he contacted the Fiji Market Authority, and with their help, Mahesh managed to ship watermelon to New Zealand at a good profit. His boss was very happy, and he give him one block of farmland for less than cost price. Mahesh and his brother-in-law, Buddy, both bought the land together. It was ten acres, and the best block in the area. Since the land was free hold property, it took time to complete the transfer. Once the land was transferred to Mahesh and Buddy, they were able to get a loan from the development bank to develop the land. The next watermelon season Mahesh planted some watermelons in his farm land as well. The two were able to make some money to pay off the loan, as well as divided some of the profits equally.

Losing Hair

Mahesh faces another big challenge when he started losing his hair. He had no idea why this was happening at such a young age. He thought this was happening because of heading the ball while playing soccer.

In Tailevu, the soccer field is muddy most of the time due to all the rain they get. And there isn't enough grass on the field. Mahesh became very worried, he did not want to lose his hair, he tried all the products on the market. Even some homemade oil. If someone give him any idea on how to keep his hair, he tried it. One person advised him to go and see a magician. He did, and it did not work. Another friend suggested that he cut his hair very short, but Mahesh did not want to do that. Mahesh had a very nice flat top head of hair from when he was working on the farm. He did not have a watch, so he estimated time by looking his shadow. Literally using his head as a sundial. In the evening, when the last bus came he knew it would be after 5pm.

Once when he was in a pharmacy he saw Cod Liver Oil on sale and realized that he had stopped taking Cod Liver oil for long time. He thought that might be the cause of losing hair, so he started taking it again. The hair did not grow back, but at least he stopped losing as much.

Convenience Store

Mahesh's brother-in-law, Buddy had a friend who was migrating overseas, and this friend owned a convenience store about ten miles east of Mahesh's house. He insisted that Mahesh and his brother-in-law purchase this store for less than market value. Buddy wanted to purchase this store together with Mahesh. When Mahesh negotiated with the owner, he agreed to sell the store on finance. He told them they didn't have to pay all the money at the same time. Mahesh and his brother-in-law buddy purchased the convenience store together. It was a very small convenience store, but in a very good location. At the corner of four road junction, there was only one other store close by, but it was not very popular.

Everyday Mahesh would have to get up very early to open the shop. His brother-in-law would come to the store after dropping the kids to school, then Mahesh would go to his sales job for the day. In the afternoon, when Mahesh finished work, he would go directly to the store to give his brother-in-law some relief. But most of the time he came very late. So,

Mahesh's wife stayed in the store because Buddy had to go to the movie theater job.

Their lives became very busy. Mahesh, his wife and his brother-in-law became very busy and did not have a lot of time for their families. On some Sunday evenings, after the store closed, Mahesh and Buddy would take their families to the beach. Mahesh's brother-in-law loved to go to the seaside for picnics. They also spent a lot of time at his other brother-in-law's house. Both families would travel together in one car, four kids and four adults. Every time they took a bottle of Gordon's gin. Those days it was very famous in Fiji. This is how they enjoyed their life.

Around that time home video cassettes came into the market. The cinema business was dying, and Buddy's theater had to close for business. He spent most of his time in the shop, and he started selling video cassettes, but in the market, people can rent a copy of a VHS tape for only one dollar per day. Now his family had only one source of income, the store. The store did not make a big profit, due to price control. And the cost of developing a farm was very high, they needed money to hire the tractor to cultivate the land. Mahesh did not want to sell the farm without making a lot of profit. The market was going up, so they decided to hold it for a bit longer.

Religious Club

Mahesh's life was very busy, and during this busy time, his neighbours wanted him to join a religious club. His neighbours were very nice to him, so that he wouldn't refuse. But Mahesh had no time to become a member. To be a member Mahesh would have to attend all the meetings, and religious functions. Mahesh offered to be the auditor of the club. He offered to audit the account books for free but did not have time to attend all of the religious functions and meetings. He explained to the club members that if he is the club's auditor, he cannot become a member. They agreed to take his offer. Mahesh became so committed to work and busy that he did not even have time to go see his parents.

Mahesh's parents lived an hour and a half drive away. Good thing Mahesh's father drove a passenger van in his hometown. So, from time to time his father and mother would come to his house to see their grandkids. Mahesh and his brothers had given some money to his parents, so that they can buy their own vehicle. His father bought a seven-seater van for himself, so that he can use this van to do some business too.

Lottery Ticket Fiji

By the mid-1980s, Mahesh and Buddy had one more child each. Mahesh had a baby boy and his brother-in-law has a baby girl. Both of the families were very happy. Their budgets were very tight though. Mahesh had no idea how his eldest daughter knew that her mom and dad did not have any money. Every time she passed by a Masjid she would say "Allah paysa dho" which meant "God give money."

Mahesh's Young Family, 1985

One day Mahesh was shopping in the video cassette store, and the store owner's son was selling a lottery ticket for his school's charity. The store owner's son insisted Mahesh buy one ticket. Mahesh bought one ticket under his daughter's name. On his next visit to the video store, the owner said to Mahesh that the ticket he purchased from his son, under his daughter's name, is a first prize winning ticket. That he should bring his daughter and ticket to claim the prize. Mahesh was a little worried; he does not think that he still had the ticket. The shop owner took Mahesh to the school principal, to make sure Mahesh got his prize. The store owner was also fighting for the prize money, because his son was entitled to get money for selling the winning ticket. IN the end it all worked out. After the school principal investigated, he wrote

Mahesh a cheque for one thousand dollars, and the store owner's son was paid for selling the winning ticket.

Mahesh used the money to purchase inventory for the shop, and for his sister's wedding. One of Mahesh's sisters was staying on the other Island called Vanua Levu. The wedding was in the major city of Labasa, where Sagan was posted. Mahesh, his wife and his parents all attended the wedding, good thing Mahesh won some money to pay for airplane tickets for everyone. Mahesh's sister liked Labasa, she is settled in Labasa still to this day.

Fiji Elections Tensions

In 1987 there was a general election in Fiji. It was historic, as it marked the first electoral transition of power in Fijian history. The long time Alliance Party was defeated by a multiracial coalition, consisting of the Fiji labour party. The economy was starting to boom and there was a large demand for farmland and houses. Because of this, Mahesh decided to list his farmland. He had some offers but did not have time to show the land and proceed with the paperwork. Finally, he got one buyer who was willing to pay double the asking price. Mahesh booked the appointment with his lawyer for the following week. And in that same week, the Fijian government was deposed in a coup D'état by Lieutenant Colonel Sitiveni Rabuka. Everything became so quiet in Fiji. Everything felt frozen, no one wanted to do any business.

Mahesh's client, the one who wanted to purchase his farmland, had disappeared. His shop became very quiet. Customers only came if they really needed something. He had to close the main door and pass the goods from the window because of all the looting. Mr. Rabuka announced that people were not allowed to stay in a group of more than five after 6pm. On Sundays all businesses were closed. Farmers weren't even allowed to milk their cows. Mr. Rabuka stated that Sunday is a holiday. He said to not do any business on Sundays.

One Sunday, Mahesh was just going to check in on his store and was stopped by two army men with guns. They told him to go back home right away and threatened to shoot him if he didn't listen. Mahesh returned home right away. He was very scared and stopped leaving his house on Sundays. Fijian Indians had no clue what would happen to them. There were rumours everywhere that the Indians would have to go back to India. It was just rumours. There was no news on the radio and they stopped the newspapers from printing. At Mahesh's workplace, only some of the staff would come to work.

During this time, Mahesh had an encounter that would change his life forever. One day, Mahesh was in the shop at his workplace, when a van full of army men accompanying Mr. Sitiveni Rabuka pulled up. He was so scared. Mahesh thought that there was going to be a big problem. But when he saw that they were smiling at him, Mahesh relaxed. A little.

Mr. Rabuka asked Mahesh if his company made beds? Mahesh replied "Yes, sir".

"How long will it take to supply five hundred beds?" Mr. Rabuka asked.

"We will do it in no time, because we are not busy." Mahesh assured him. Mr. Rabuka gave him an order for five hundred beds without even asking the price. Mahesh's boss was very happy, but a little worried about the payment. Mahesh told his manager that they didn't really have a choice, because if he refused the order, Mr. Rabuka might close down his factory.

Within a week's time Mahesh shipped the first order. It was sold at double the regular price. Mahesh thought that there was no way they would pay for the order. When Mahesh went to ask for the payment he was very scared. He went to their office and asked for the payment. He was so surprised to see the cheque. Mahesh got the cheque without any questions asked, and they placed another order for the same amount. One of the officers gave Mahesh his card and told him that if he ever encountered an army barrack, or if anyone stopped him, just show them his card.

One day, Mahesh had to go pick up his manager's passport from the government passport office. He ended up being stopped by two army men at gunpoint. Mahesh showed them the card he had from the officer. He told them to call the officer, as the card had his direct number. They let him go. Mahesh kept this card with him always.

Meeting in Sakuna Park

Mahesh was getting nervous about not hearing much on the political situation in Fiji. He heard that there was going to be a public meeting in Sakuna Park in Suva and planned on attending with his family to see if he can find out more about what is going to happen in Fiji.

Mahesh was on his way to attend the meeting, but Master stopped him. Not because his cousin did not want Mahesh attending the meeting, but because he needed a partner to play cards with. After a couple hours of playing cards, Mahesh decided to head to the meeting with his family. Mahesh almost reached Sukuna Park when he saw many cars coming the other way at a fast speed, blowing their horns and yelling at him to go back. During the meeting, a huge fight broke out between the Native Fijians and the Fijian Indians. Everyone was trying to leave the park; finally, one of the drivers gave him way to turn his car around and out of danger.

Mahesh was very scared for his family's safety. Many Fijian Indians were leaving the country. Back then, Fijians did not need to travel with a holiday Visa when travelling to Australia, New Zealand or Canada. The immigration departments would just stamp their passports on arrival. Many people took advantage of this and moved out to Australia, New Zealand, and Canada, on tourist Visas.

Immigrating to Canada

Roughly six months later, Mahesh's brother-in-law from Canada found out that a lot of Fijians were coming to Canada on tourist Visas and applying for "refugee" status afterwards. Mahesh's brother-in-law called Mahesh and explained everything to him. He told Mahesh that if he wanted to come to Canada, they had a place ready for them, but there was no guarantee that he would be granted permanent resident status in Canada. This was the first time Mahesh ever heard the word "refugee". He needed to make sure that this was the right thing to do, so he went to his manager for advice. His manager told him, "If someone was willing to take care of you and your family, you should take your chances."

His manager didn't understand why Mahesh wouldn't want to go. He assured Mahesh that if he ever had to come back to Fiji, he would always have a job in his company. Mahesh's manager was also planning on leaving to New Zealand until everything settled down. Mahesh called his brother in Australia for some help and advice as well.

Mahesh's brother agreed with the manager, he thought that because of the situation in Fiji there is a good chance that he would be granted to stay in Canada. Mahesh's brother even gave him some money to help pay for airplane tickets for his family.

With the advice of some of his most trusted family and friends, Mahesh was now determined to follow-through on this plan to move to Canada.

Since he was trying to leave Fiji immediately, Mahesh would not need his car anymore, and he needed help selling it. Raven, the troublemaker from his childhood, actually grew up to become a police officer. This cousin grew up on a farm, just like Mahesh. After he saw everyone move out of Tailevu, he tried hard to become a police officer. He was now in a very high position. He told Mahesh that he would help him sell his car to another policeman. Mahesh did not want to give the car to anyone without getting at least some money in return, but he told his friend that if he could not sell the car, then his younger brother can take it for free.

Mahesh was completely invested into his plan on moving to Canada; however, he did not want to leave Buddy behind. Mahesh told his brother-in-law to get ready, they are leaving for Canada. His brother-in-law asked when they would be leaving. Mahesh replied as soon as we get the flight, may be as soon as two days. But when Mahesh and his brother-in-law went to the travel agent to buy airline tickets, all the flights were fully booked. The first available flight being one month away. They had no choice, Mahesh bought the tickets for both families.

While they were waiting for their flight date to arrive, the Canadian Immigration Office announced that anyone travelling to Canada must have a Visa. To help accommodate people who are going to travel to Canada they set up a temporary immigration office in the city of Nadi, right next to the airport. This was on the west side of the Fiji Islands. Mahesh and his brother-in-law lived on the east side.

In those days, you didn't just go line up first come first serve, you had to wait for your appointment date. Since they had already bought their tickets, Mahesh and Buddy were worried they wouldn't get an appointment in time. When they found out about their appointment date, they were relieved. Their appointment was set for two days before their flight, so they wouldn't have to cancel their flight. The Immigration officer told them not to bring their families for the interview, just their passports. The appointment had a date, but no time. They just said to come on this day.

Mahesh and his brother-in-law drove to Nadi to get the Visa. There were army men all over the place, a lot of checkpoints. Luckily Mahesh had the card from the army man he met a few months ago. Every time he would get stopped, he showed them that card.

It was not easy to get the Visa. As soon as they reached the office they could see that there were a lot of people waiting. There was a large group of people just waiting outside of the office. The majority of the people seemed to be getting rejected. Mahesh and his brother-in-law were confident though, as they went fully prepared. Their travel agent had educated them on what to say. Mahesh had to make it look like they were going to Canada for a vacation, and not trying to flee Fiji. You have to look like you have money. So, to help him out Mahesh's manager made a money order for a large amount for him to deposit, so it looked like they really were going for a holiday. Mahesh's brother-in-law brought his father's bank book and would say that it was his. His father recently sold his house, so there was a pretty good balance.

When they reached The Canadian Immigration office, they were not allowed to go directly inside. The security officer collected everyone's documents, and only the selected people were called inside the office. Most of them got their papers returned by the security officer and told to leave. It was after 4pm, just before closing time. Mahesh said to Buddy that he thinks they won't be called that day, and maybe they'll give them an appointment the next morning. They were getting really anxious, and then right when they were losing hope, the security officer called them in for their interview.

Mahesh and Buddy were both called in for the interview at the same time. The immigration officer asked them if they ever visited Canada before, Mahesh replied yes in 1982, for a holiday. The officer asked if he traveled by himself, again Mahesh replied yes. He told the officer that they were planning to take their family to see a white Christmas. And they found out that this is the right time for that, and that his business has slowed down right now, so the timing was perfect. Next thing they heard was "Have a nice holiday in Canada."

OH MY GOD!!! This was the happiest moment in Mahesh's life. As soon as they came out of the office, Mahesh jumped up and down so many times. Mahesh told his brother-in-law, that his dreams are coming true. Mahesh's cousin Master, who also went with them, saw Mahesh and Buddy coming towards him laughing; he could tell by their faces that they got the Visas.

They were so happy on the drive back, happily drinking beer. They didn't have cell phones to call their family and tell the good news. Everyone was waiting to hear back from them. Mahesh could not wait to tell his family that they got the Visa and to start packing. When they arrived home, it was night time, but no one was sleeping, they were waiting for their arrival. As soon as they arrived home, everyone asked Mahesh, if he got the Visa. They were so happy to find out that they got their Visas that they were all jumping with joy.

Mahesh's wife was so confident, she had already started packing earlier that day. Later they found out only three families got their Visas that day.

The next morning Mahesh called his parents and told them that they got the Visa for Canada. And that their flight was the following evening, but they had to go to the airport early in the morning. Mahesh's parents came right away and started helping them pack. His parents were very sad and emotional, they thought they were never going to see their son and his family again. When Mahesh saw them, he felt very sad. He felt like cancelling the Canada Visa, but at the same time, he thought about his dream and his family.

Flight to Canada

The next day, his parents wanted to go with them to the airport. Mahesh refused because it was very dangerous to travel that far. The army was all over the place, with very aggressive checkpoints. When they were ready to leave the house, Mahesh saw his sister-in-law packing all their dishes and cutlery to take with them to Canada. Mahesh asked her what she was doing and told her to leave everything behind. He told her that they are not supposed to look like they are migrating to Canada. They have to look like they are just going on a holiday. Buddy became nervous and didn't want to travel with them anymore. Mahesh yelled at them to just leave everything behind except their clothes. Mahesh demanded that they come with him. Mahesh was always the decision maker, and everyone listened to him. Mahesh knew that everything in the house will be taken care of by his wife's brother, who was not leaving for Canada or the United States. Mahesh told Buddy that if we have to come back, we can go back to living in our houses. It was still a very difficult decision for them to make, but they've come so far. Mahesh was always a risk taker, and he knew that without taking any risks you won't become successful.

They arrived at the airport five hours before their flight time. They were stopped so many times by military checkpoints. The airport was jammed packed when they got there. The army was all over the place. Nobody talked to each other as they were standing in the lineups. Right when Mahesh was about to reach the counter, an army man came and opened all of his luggage. Mahesh had to close the bags by himself and then an airline officer came and opened the bags again. After finishing at the counter, the security officer re-checked everything. It took more than three hours to reach the boarding area. Mahesh looked calm but, in his mind, he was very nervous, he knew anything could happen. They were waiting in the boarding area when they heard an announcement that their flight was delayed. Mahesh's brother-in-law asked him if everything was under control. He just confirmed that it's just a flight delay, telling him to try and stay close to Mahesh, and act normal. After one hour, the boarding started. Everyone was rushing to get in first, but Mahesh and his brother-in-law's families were allowed to board first, because they were travelling with small children. As soon as the flight took off, Mahesh was so relieved. He went up to his brother-in-law with two glasses of wine in his hands, laughing and saying my dreams are coming true.

Everyone was relaxed but very tired and hungry. They could not wait for the food to arrive. Within one hour they were served a delicious dinner. Before landing in Hawaii, the captain announced that the connecting flight to Los Angeles (LA) will be delayed for two hours. Mahesh's brother-in-law came to him again told him that he thinks that they were on the wrong plane. Mahesh told him not to worry, he knew they will switch to another plane after landing in LA. Getting to Canada was the only thing on Mahesh's mind, and he knew that they would have a few stops along the way.

They were running into delays their whole trip, while waiting to board in LA, there was another announcement, the flight to Toronto was delayed by one hour. Finally, they boarded the plane in LA, from there it took five hours to land in Toronto.

December 6, 1987

The Canadian immigration and customs officers were very nice. They just collected all their documents without checking any luggage and told Mahesh and his family "Please go this way out." Mahesh became worried because there was no door, and the officers did not ask any questions. The person behind him said "Go, go you're done," and as soon as Mahesh moved, the wall opened up by itself. Mahesh had never seen a wall open by itself before. And written in big letters were the words "WELCOME TO CANADA." Mahesh was so happy. And then another door opened up, it was like a freezer. It was minus twenty with gusting wind that day, and when he looked back, the door behind them was closing. And written on it in big letters was "DO NOT ENTER."

Mahesh had no idea what to do, but then he saw his brother-in-law from Toronto, with big heavy coats calling him to come. The families all greeted each other and cried. All while loading all of their luggage quickly as possible, and bundling up in the jackets, as it was so cold. They packed up the cars and were off to start their new lives in Canada.

After more than one hour of driving, his brother-in-law finally stopped, and said "You are home now." There was one foot of snow in the driveway, it felt very cold because they did not wear winter boots, they only had dress shoes. The kids loved it though, they started playing with the snow right away. This was the first time his kids had seen snow. Mahesh felt so cold, he told his wife, "I will never forget this date in my life. December 06, 1987."

Once inside the house, they went straight to the basement. The basement was nice and warm, this was something new for Mahesh. A basement. A room underground. When Mahesh went to Edmonton, everyone stayed in high rise apartments.

First month in Toronto
– December 1987

While living in Canada, Mahesh tried to learn as much as he could about Canada. He learned that it is the second largest country in the world. Canada has more lakes than the rest of the world. And that Toronto is the biggest City in Canada.

For more than one month they stayed in the basement. Only sometimes Mahesh would go out if his brother-in-law went shopping, especially if he went to purchase liquor from the LCBO. Mahesh came with three hundred of Fiji dollars, he thought this was enough money for some time, but when he started purchasing some goods for his kids, the money was moving out so fast. It was a good thing that they stayed in his brother-in-law's basement, they did not have to pay rent or buy groceries. Mahesh and Bijma would go shopping for only small items for the kids.

Mahesh's wife's older brother, took care of his family, they bought winter clothes for everyone. It was the Christmas season, so relatives and friends always came to his brother-in-law's house for parties. They had parties every time someone would visit. Mahesh's brother-in-law was a very happy and lively person. He had another, younger brother, who lived 10 minutes away from his house, and every time he came over, the party started. Bijma's older brother's wife had four brothers in Toronto too. They were within an hour drive from where he was staying, and on the weekends when they came, the party was on.

Even though he was having a lot of fun in Canada, Mahesh missed Christmas in Fiji. Over here they spent Christmas in the basement, just drinking and eating exactly like they did the day before. In Fiji, most of the time they stayed outside, killed a goat or chicken, chicken for sure, and they would go to their relatives' homes to exchange gifts, then at night the party started.

Living in Canada: Immigration process

After the first month they all went to see the immigration lawyer to apply for refugee status. The lawyer explained that since they came for a holiday, that while they are still on their holiday they could not apply for refugee status. The lawyer told them to come back after their three-month holiday Visa was expired, and then he would give them a letter to take to the immigration office. The Lawyer charged Mahesh five hundred dollars and another five hundred dollars to his brother-in-law's family. They both did not have this kind of money, so they took a loan from Mahesh's wife's brother.

The holiday Visa was for three months. Three months was a long time for them to stay in the basement, as it was getting very boring down there. As soon as the weather became a little better, Mahesh would go out to see some of the neighbours and talk to them. Though Mahesh would get confused every time he spoke to them. He did not know what to say at what time. In Fiji they said "Bula, bula" for every greeting. Over here, it's "Good morning", "Good afternoon", "Good evening", or "Good night".

Mahesh was not sure what to say on cold snowy days, "Bad day?" One day it was nice weather, so Mahesh went to his neighbor, and said to him "good morning what a nice day". The neighbour replied, "What? It is a gorgeous morning. It is spring." Mahesh thought oh, in spring, we have to say "Gorgeous morning."

After the three months had passed, they went to the same lawyer to get the letter. The lawyer charged another five hundred again to each family just to open the case, gave them a letter and said take this letter to the immigration officer. Lawyer told them he did not have to be there at this time.

Mahesh went to the immigration office with his brother-in-law from Toronto, but didn't get a chance to see the immigration officer, because their quota was filled. The security officer told them that they have to come early in the morning if they want to see the officer. The security officer repeated, "I mean very early between 5am and 6am, and stand in the line outside. Before 8am one of the security officers will come and give everyone a ticket, and you have to proceed with your ticket. And if you are late you have to come again."

So next morning, Mahesh and his brother-in-law woke up very early, about 4am, and reached downtown at about 6am. They thought they would be the first people there, but when they got to the office, they saw more than twenty people already standing in line. Mahesh, Bijma and his brother-in-law went and stood at the end of the lineup.

Waiting in the line was not easy, because the weather was very cold that day, it was minus fifteen degrees. Good thing they did not have to bring their kids. Thank God there was a coffee shop next to the immigration office building. Mahesh and his brother-in-law took turns standing in line, and going in the coffee shop. They did this to keep warm until the security officer came and gave them a number.

After the door opened everyone went inside and waited for their number to be called. In the afternoon the office was about to close. Mahesh and Bijma have been waiting all day when one of the lady immigration officers called Mahesh's number. After a long conversation with the officer, Mahesh and Bijma were told that they were not refugees; they have come as tourists. Mahesh showed her the letter given by his lawyer and told her they were coming as refugees, but at the last moment, they had to take the holiday Visa. The lady officer discussed with her senior officer and decided to accept their application. The lady officer told Mahesh, the letter from the lawyer was nothing. They did not need the letter. But the immigration officer accepted Mahesh's application, and he had to come again. Mahesh asked the officer, if they had to line up again or come directly to her. The immigration officer replied, 'You have to line up, and any of the officers can consult with you.'

Before the next visit Mahesh called his lawyer and told him that they needed him to come, because immigration officer's English was very hard to understand. The lawyer advised him to take his time and answer the questions. The lawyer told Mahesh that he would go with them for his hearing, but it wouldn't be for a long time. The lawyer advised Mahesh to tell the officer the same story Mahesh told him. That the army gave him a very hard time, that he spent a night in jail, just because he went to see his father on a Sunday. That his family is not safe in Fiji, the kids have to go to a school that is far from their house. The lawyer then said to give his letter to the immigration officer. Mahesh told the lawyer his letter was not needed, and how he did not understand why he gave him one thousand dollars. The lawyer replied to Mahesh "You will need me for sure."

When the day came, Mahesh and Bijma had to leave early in the morning, just like the last time. They had to take two buses, and the subway, then walk before reaching the immigration office building, and wait in line. This time when he was called, there was a different immigration officer. And he was a very nice officer. He took all the documents and all the information again. The officer gave Mahesh the papers for his kids to attend school, and gave him another date to meet within three months.

Now, Mahesh felt lucky, maybe his dream was coming true. Mahesh did not have any money left, good thing his wife got a part time cash job, cooking. Mahesh's brother-in-law had a part time cleaning business, so Mahesh sometimes goes with his brother-in-law to help him, because they were staying in his basement without paying rent and not even paying money for food. The budget was getting very tough day-by-day. The kids were in school, and Mahesh's brother-in-law had just listed his house for sale. Mahesh and his family had to move out within three months. It was good news that the Government of Canada announced that all the refugees would get work permits, so they can work in Canada. On the next visit to the immigration office, Mahesh was called by the same officer and he and his wife got a work permit.

Real Estate Licence

Mahesh was feeling very lucky and thought his dream was coming true. Mahesh started working through an agency as a laborer. He did not like to do this type of work but the kids were in school, and he had to pay all the credit he borrowed from his relatives. His brother from Melbourne, Australia loaned him some money when he was coming to Canada. Mahesh continued working and decided to attend school for some courses, he did not want to do the labour job for the rest of his life. The best choice was a real estate course at Centennial College, because he had some experience from Fiji. Mahesh sold farm land in Fiji. So, he had some experience with how to deal with lawyers and register the property. And Centennial College was not very far from his house, he could walk down to college. One day Mahesh got a ride with his sister-in-law to Centennial College and got registered for the real estate course.

The Toronto Real Estate Board (TREB) is Canada's largest real estate board. The majority of real estate transactions make use of Toronto Real Estate Board. To get an Ontario

Real Estate licence, three courses and exams are required, for pre-registration. Mahesh registered for the courses through Centennial College as a full-time student while doing night shift work. He did not have a lot of time to study for his exam, and on his first attempt, he did not pass. The exam was multiple choice, he has never seen this type of question before. To continue, he had to wait for two weeks, but he had an opportunity to proceed from another location of Centennial College. Mahesh registered for those courses but this time it was evening session, and he had to go by bus. After studying hard, he passed the first level in three weeks. He took evening sessions again because he got full time employment in the warehouse for a company who got a subcontract with Canada Post. Mahesh's duty was sorting expedited parcels, he liked it for the time being and he continued studying for his real estate licence.

Mahesh and his family had to move out from his brother-in-law's house, because his brother-in-law was selling his house. Mahesh with his family moved to a one-bedroom basement apartment. The kids had to sleep in the veranda. Mahesh had to take a bus to school and work, not very far from the new address. Mahesh continued studying and working at the same, time but he did not pass the second level exam, but he did not want to give up. Mahesh changed the location for the college and registered again to complete the courses on the second attempt. This time, he passed the level two exam. For the level three he had to wait for three weeks. After three weeks he registered again to complete the course for real estate, this time he studied very hard to pass the exam, and he did. He received his real estate licence from Toronto Real Estate Board, within three weeks of hard study.

The Real Estate Council of Ontario, (RECO) regulates real estate salespeople. You had to register under the brokerage within one year of receiving the certificate. To register under the broker you must reside in Canada for more than one year as a permanent resident. Mahesh had resided in Canada for more than one year, but as a refugee with work permit. Mahesh went to one of the brokers and submitted his certificate and explained about his status. The broker told him the Real Estate Council of Ontario may accept his application, because he has a work permit and have been working in Canada for more than one year. Mahesh submitted the application to the ministry for registration, the application was declined. The ministry indicated that it could be reconsidered after Mahesh becomes permanent resident of Canada. By the time Mahesh got his permanent residence of Canada, the registration time had expired, and he would have to redo all the exams again.

First Halloween

October 1988 was their first Halloween. Mahesh had no idea what Halloween was. In Fiji they did not celebrate Halloween. Some of his colleagues told Mahesh to take his kids on the street after 6pm, and people will give them sweets. Mahesh thought maybe some people will give one or two candies. Bijma was working that night, so he gathered his three kids, and told them "Come let's go out, you might get some sweets." They went out after 6pm, on the same street were they staying. Mahesh's thought they might get some candies, so they went to a house that was decorated with lights. All of his kids got nice candies, and chips, they were very happy. They went to the next house, and the lady noticed that the kids didn't have any bags with them. She went back inside and, Mahesh told the kids to come back and get ready to go home. He thought they got their treats, and they were done for the night.

Then, just when they were about to head home, the lady came back out, and started calling them to come to her, "Come, I have bags for everyone!" She gave nice chocolates, chips, and candy to everyone. She asked them, "Is this your first Halloween?" The kids said "Yes!" She told them "Keep going to every house, you will get a lot of candy." In an hour's time all the kids collected more than half a plastic bag full of candy. Mahesh was shocked, he never thought people would give away nice sweets for free.

First Diwali in Canada

November 1988. This was Mahesh's first Diwali in Canada. It was stormy in Toronto. With heavy winds, and flurries. Mahesh tried to light diyas outside, but it was very difficult. His family sat inside without fireworks or candles, because those were not allowed inside the house.

Mahesh thought about when he was a small boy. Diwali was very special for them. His father would buy new clothes for everyone. The family would light candles and diyas outside. His mom would be busy cooking nice food and sweets all day. He used to play outside all day with fireworks. At night, Mahesh's father would put Mahesh's brother, Sagan, on his shoulders, hold Mahesh's hand, and take them in the village to see the lights.

Sagan asked, "Daddy, why there is a lot of water on the ground?" His father replied, "Son, today is Saturday and Diwali, and whenever it is very dark, especially on Diwali, it is very high tide. Sometimes big fish and sharks come from the sea during high tide."

Mahesh thought about his dad's joke. He knew his dad was lying, but he thought it was very funny that his brother believed him. Since that day, Sagan got scared when there was high tide on Saturdays. He would never go close to the river – on Saturdays. One of the pundits also told him that he specifically would have high risk from the water and sharks, since he did not know how to swim. When all the kids were diving in the river, he would fill his bucket full of water, from the river and take his bath.

Although he was determined to chase his dream in Canada, it was hard not thinking about being back home.

Job at Canada Post and new rental home

Mahesh started liking the work he was doing for Canada Post once he was hired directly, and no longer with an agency. Everything was going well. However, Mahesh found out that his brother in law, Buddy, was not feeling well. The basement apartment he was renting was very old and cold. Mahesh told his brother-in-law that he needs to move out from this basement. Mahesh told him that he will look for a house, and they can all move in there together. Mahesh found a four-bedroom house in the same neighborhood, and told his brother-in-law, that he will rent this property, and they can move in this house and split the rent. This may help him get better, because the apartment he was renting is very cold. His brother-in-law agreed to move in with him.

First Diwali at their rental home.

Mahesh's manager wanted to promote him to lead hand, but Mahesh would need to improve his computer knowledge. Mahesh registered for an Introduction to Computer Applications course at the DeVry Institute of Technology. DeVry was for-profit college and training school. It eventually became DeVry University. Mahesh completed the stage one course within two months. He wanted to go for the stage two course, but Mahesh did not proceed because of the high fees, and did not have enough time to do the all-day courses.

Stage one was enough to help Mahesh get promoted to lead hand, so continuing wasn't absolutely necessary either. As lead hand, his duties included hiring part time staff to sort expedited parcels. Mahesh usually hired high school students, and family members who needed to work part time. The majority of people came from agencies. Mahesh also operated the forklift to load and unload containers from tractor trailers.

Mahesh would always remember one of his most embarrassing moments at work. The night supervisor approached Mahesh and told him that the conveyor belt was not running properly and made some type of noise. The supervisor asked Mahesh to call someone to get it fixed. Mahesh thought he should check on it first.

Mahesh went to the machine and turned off the switch and opened the motor cover and saw the motor's chain was a little loose. Mahesh decided to fix it himself. He adjusted the screw and very carefully turned the belt back on. The belt was running properly, so he turned it off again and put the cover back with caution. Mahesh was always talked about safety with his crew, so he knew he had to move carefully and slowly.

When Mahesh turned on the belt again, it was still making a little sound. The chain was touching the cover. Mahesh turned off the switch again and opened the cover for more adjustment. After Mahesh fully adjusted the chain, he went and turned it back on again. He decided to use his left-hand index finger to check out how loose the chain was. In a second, the tip of his finger was sliced. It wasn't very painful, but it was very embarrassing for Mahesh. He always talked about safety to his colleagues. Mahesh could not understand how he could make this kind of a mistake.

However, that was not as bad as one of the biggest mistakes Mahesh had ever made at that job. Mahesh's forklift operator did not come to work, so Mahesh had to operate the forklift himself. He was loading and unloading the containers from the tractor trailer. As he was loading a mono trainer in the trailer. By mistake he went into a trailer that was about to move out of the dock. Mahesh was inside the trailer, when he realized that this trailer is moving out, as soon as he backed his forklift out of the trailer, the driver pulled the trailer out of the dock quickly. If Mahesh stayed in the trailer for one more second, he could have died. For five minutes Mahesh was in shock and did not move. He just kept thinking about what he just did.

"New" Car

Mahesh's budget was very tight, but he really needed a car. The first car he bought was a four door Alliance Standard. He bought it for just eight hundred dollars, because it was manual, and needed the clutch plate to be changed. Mahesh knew that he and his nephew could do it by themselves. After changing the clutch plate, Mahesh drove this car from Toronto to Niagara Falls with his family, but forgot to change the tires, two of the tires were on the canvas. This was another big mistake that he made in his life. Changing the flat tires on the highway, he had to do this twice, luckily, the highway was not that busy and he got his family home safely.

One day this car broke down. Mahesh asked Buddy to pull the car to Canadian Tire for repairs. They didn't get a tow truck, they just tied the car to Buddy's car with a cable or rope, and he pulled it to Canadian tire. Mahesh sat in the broken down car, applying the brakes and turning the wheel if he had to. When his brother-in-law was pulling the car, he was supposed to look back to check on Mahesh, but he was not looking back.

While they were on their way to Canadian Tire, the car's windows became stuck, the brakes were also not working, even the horn was not working. Mahesh could not get Buddy's attention to stop him from pulling the car. Finally, when his brother-in-law stopped at a red light, Mahesh jumped out to talk to his brother-in-law. He wanted to tell him to go very slow, but as soon as he got out of the car, the light turned green, and his brother-in-law took off again without looking back. Mahesh ran and jumped back in the car. Good thing the door was unlocked. When they reached Canadian Tire, Mahesh became a little relaxed, and told his brother-in-law what happened when he was pulling the car. Mahesh ended up paying a lot of money to repair this car, because the onboard computer was down. Mahesh didn't even know that cars had a computer.

Son's acting Hobby

Mahesh's son, Vishal, was very much interested to act in movies. Because of this Mahesh took him to a children's acting school to do some formal training to become an actor. The school was in downtown Toronto, it was known as a great training centre for children in Toronto. They trained him in acting and modeling in front of a camera and on-stage. The training was an eighteen-week program on Saturdays.

Mahesh and his wife would have to take Vishal downtown every weekend and wait for him while he attended the classes. He was around eleven years old at the time. After he completed the training school, they had to look for an agency that his son could work with. The school didn't do this for their students, but they did give referrals for a few. Mahesh found an agency that they can work with. They assured them that they would find jobs for Vishal, but they would need twenty 12"x 8" colour photos of him, and would also have to pay some fees to enrol his son. Vishal was very much interested to become an actor so Mahesh decided to help his son pursue his dream.

It ended up working out well for them. The agency found many roles for his son, but usually as a background performer and small roles in TV shows, movies and commercials. The first movie he was in starred Wesley Snipes, it was the movie called *Murder at 1600*. This was just a small background role as an extra, but everyone was excited for Vishal. He went on to do this for many years. Mahesh's son ended up getting a few small roles that led to ACTRA credits, but nothing that resulted in a big acting career. He still had a lot of fun when going to the shoots. Whenever Vishal had a role in a movie or commercial, Mahesh or Bijma would have to stay on site as children could not be left on set without a parent.

Learning to Skate

After living in Canada for a few years, Mahesh started to get interested in skating and really wanted to learn how to skate. He decided to go to the recreation centre to find out how to enrol into lessons. He was told that he needed to bring his own skates, and that the fees were 50 cents per lesson, which was a pretty good price. Mahesh bought new skates and started going to the recreation centre to learn to skate. There wasn't any one-on-one instructor time, it was a group lesson. Mahesh fell so many times, until one lady instructor came over to him and showed him how to get up. Sometimes they would come and give some ideas on how to stop, and turn yourself, but most of the time you're on your own. Mahesh did not give up skating, and within two to three months he learned how to skate. Every evening after work, Mahesh would go to Scarborough Town Centre to skate, because it was a free outdoor public rink.

Potential Canada Post Strike

In 1990, Canada Post and the Canadian Union of Postal Workers (CUPW) had been in contract negotiations and about 50,000 postal workers went on strike.

At Mahesh's workplace, his duty was to hire part time employees, mostly from an agency. Sometimes Mahesh would hire his relatives' and friends' adult children to sort expedited parcels. When Canada Post workers went on strike, it went longer than expected. Mahesh was using his crew to sort emergency parcels in different locations during the night. Somehow the union leader found out their location, and one night he came and locked everyone inside the building. The next morning when Mahesh saw the door, the gate was chained with heavy locks. He could not go inside, and trucks were not allowed in or out. When Mahesh went to talk to the people on the picket line, he was almost beaten by them. Mahesh was an easygoing person, and was able to handle this situation. He was very friendly with them, and was able to negotiate with their leader to let him go inside. Mahesh was allowed to go inside, but they did not allow any of the workers to go home. Those days Mahesh did not have access to a cell phone to order food for his workers, and it was almost lunch time. They did not have breakfast either.

It was a Sunday morning and the agency was closed. Mahesh went back to the picket line and tried to talk with the union workers again. He sweet-talked them into allowing him to get food. Mahesh offered to bring food for everyone, including the union workers at the picket line. They allowed him to and he went and bought pizza for everyone. At the end of the day everyone was released. Mahesh's supervisor and managers were very pleased with the way he controlled the situation.

The managers from Canada Post found a secluded warehouse in a rural area between residential neighbourhoods, two hours away from the city since the other location was found out. One night, Mahesh was operating a forklift to offload containers from tractor trailers coming from outside of the city. After midnight, there was a heavy knock on the door. When Mahesh opened the door, there were two policemen. They forced their way inside the warehouse. One of the officers asked Mahesh what he was doing this late in the night, people were complaining about the noise. Mahesh explained to the police officer, he was unloading the containers for Canada Post, because they are on strike. The officer asked for his identification. Mahesh did not have one, his brother-in-law took his car and his wallet was in the car. The officers told him to cut the noise, it's late at night, and people need to sleep. Mahesh had to unload the rest of the containers without his forklift, and used a hand pump to reduce the noise. The next morning he heard the strike was over.

Buying Their First House

After a few years living with his brother in law and his family, a real estate agent spoke to Mahesh and asked him why he and his brother-in-law were still renting? He told him that paying rent was just wasting money. Mahesh agreed with the real estate agent, and told him that it was because they did not have permanent residency in Canada. He asked him to come again when he gets his Visa to stay in Canada. The agent told Mahesh that he knew a broker that could help arrange a mortgage for them. The real estate agent said to Mahesh, "First, let's find the house."

The agent told Mahesh that they have to find a house that is best for him and Buddy, and within their budget. Mahesh went with the agent and searched for a property within the same neighborhood. They found a five bedroom, back split house with a finished basement. They went to the mortgage broker, who arranged the mortgage with the very best rate available. And in three months, they moved into their new house. The kids were very happy because they did not have to fight for the television, and there were a lot of space for them to play.

The immigration officer and the lawyer always wanted him to come and update the file. When Mahesh went to see the immigration officer, he mentioned the real estate property they purchased. The immigration officer suggested that he change his status from refugee to humanitarian ground status, for a better chance. The officer said to Mahesh it will speed up the processing of your case. The immigration officer gave him all the documents to complete and submit.

After completing these documents, Mahesh took them to his lawyer. Mahesh's lawyer took all of the documents and said to leave them with him. And that he will check the papers and submit them to the immigration office by himself. The lawyer also told Mahesh he will speak to the immigration officer to expedite his case. In three months' time, Mahesh received a letter from the immigration office, that they did not receive any documents. Mahesh was very upset and worried, he went to his lawyer's office to find out about the documents. The receptionist took him to the lawyer's room and asked him to wait in his office as the lawyer was busy.

Mahesh noticed his file was on the table and the documents that needed to be submitted to the immigration office was still in the file. After half an hour, when the lawyer came Mahesh asked him why he didn't submit his documents to the immigration office? The lawyer started giving some excuses. Mahesh and his lawyer had a big heated argument, and finally, Mahesh decided to proceed with his case by himself without a lawyer. Mahesh collected all the documents from his lawyer and told him, "We don't need you anymore."

Every time Mahesh went to see this lawyer, the receptionist asked for money. He had paid a lot of money and the lawyer did nothing for him. The lawyer did not attend any meeting and Mahesh asked for all the money to be refunded, his lawyer told him that they don't refund money, if you need me I will proceed with your case. Mahesh said, "I do not need you, I will proceed without you."

The next day Mahesh went to the immigration office by himself. He got in line early in the morning and went inside to submit the documents. He explained to the immigration officer why the documents were not submitted. The officer was very nice and understood Mahesh's situation. He told him that for immigration purposes, you can proceed with your case without a lawyer, it is not necessary to have a lawyer. The immigration officer booked another appointment for Mahesh to come and see him directly, so he did not need to wait in line. This officer always gave Mahesh an appointment to see him. After three or four meetings with the same officer, he said to Mahesh, "Your next visit may be your last visit." And he gave Mahesh some more forms to complete and scheduled his next appointment in two weeks.

Mahesh was worried about the outcome. When he and Bijma went to see the officer on his next appointment, the immigration officer collected all of the documents, and asked them to wait. After a few minutes, he came out frustrated, and told them that Mahesh did not complete the forms completely. Mahesh and his wife became very scared and worried, then the officer said to them, "You have ten minutes to complete these forms. I am going for coffee, if you do not finish by then, you may have to wait for another year." It was little relief for them that he allowed them to complete the forms there, but his wife was visibly annoyed with Mahesh for not completing the forms. Mahesh quickly completed the forms before the officer came back, there were just a few details missing. The officer came out with a happy face and brought them in his office.

Finally, Mahesh and his wife were granted permanent residency in Canada. This was one of the happiest days of his life. His dream was coming true, he was feeling lucky now. Mahesh had big dreams, he wanted his own house, an office on the top floor with glass windows, and his own time to come and go from his office, a reserved parking spot for his car. Sometimes he himself thought that this was not possible. Mahesh's friends and relatives laughed at him when he talked about his dream, and he would say "Nothing is impossible." He knew that he will achieve his dream one day.

Trip Back Home to Fiji

After all the hard work and running between lawyers and the immigration office, Mahesh was finally relieved. His family insisted that he take a break, and go for a holiday in Fiji. He did not have enough money for airfare, and all of the other expenses. So, Mahesh and his wife went to the bank to get a loan. Those days the branch manager would decide the loan approval. They went to see the branch manager and explained the hard times they went through and paid all the loans they got from their families. Mahesh explained to the bank manager that they don't have a high credit limit on their credit card, because most of their money was used to pay for lawyer fees. Mahesh and his wife asked the bank manager to help them, and she went to talk to her manager. Her manager was a nice person, he understood, but he said to them that your income did not qualify for any loan at this time. Bijma manager they have been working so hard for so many years, and paid all of the loans they took from friends and relatives only the credit card had a balance, but it was a small amount, which they could pay in no time. The bank manager did some adjustments to their income, and since both of them were employed full-time, they approved for a $5000 loan. Mahesh and Bijma were so happy.

Mahesh and his wife went to see a travel agent to book a flight to Fiji. The agent said all the flights are via Los Angeles, where there would be an eight hours stopover. This flight was cheap, but they needed an American Visa. They bought the tickets, and they went to the American Consulate to get the Visa. Everyone was very excited to go back to Fiji. They did a lot of shopping for their family in Fiji, and also packed a lot of gifts for them.

Finally, it was time for the family to travel to Fiji. But first, they had a layover in the US. This was Mahesh and his family's first time in America. He did not know any family or friends in Los Angeles, where they can go and spend some time. Mahesh decided to take a taxi to the nearest shopping mall. They went to one mall not very far from the airport, and did some small shopping and had lunch. They came back to the airport in a taxi two hours before their flight. The flight was on time from Los Angeles to Nadi, Fiji.

When they arrived in Fiji it was 5am in the morning. They took a taxi all the way to Tailevu. Home. Mahesh did not tell his parents that they were coming back home for a visit. When they reached the old farm home, he told his kids to walk up to the house on their own as a practical joke, because he knew is parents would not recognize them. His parents saw some kids walking towards the house, and had no idea who these kids were. Finally, Mahesh and Bijma got out of the car and everyone realized who they were. Mahesh's parents and family were so happy and surprised to see them.

The kids liked Fiji very much, because they had a lot of time to play on the farm, and swim in the river with their cousins. Mahesh visited his friends and families.

One day, Mahesh took his family to Suva City. In front of the Governor General's house at the front of the gate, there were two guards standing with large rifles. These were the types of rifles that would have a sharp knife or bayonet at the end. Mahesh's second daughter, Poonam who was 10 at the time, ran across the road, and touched the pointy end. Mahesh quickly ran and grabbed her. Luckily, the guard did not say anything. When Mahesh asked his daughter, why she did that. She replied, "I wanted to know if it was real or not." Mahesh laughed at his daughter, "Don't do that, we are not in Canada."

Mahesh took his family to his previous workplace, where he used to work before immigrating to Canada. Mahesh's manager was happy to see him and wanted Mahesh to know how much his business changed. The manager said to Mahesh "I have expanded my business, and now I have shops all over Fiji. Every city, and town you can see my shop, known as Big Bear. And in some cities I have more than one store, but I couldn't find someone like you to look after my business." Mahesh's friend, the owner of Big Bear, said "I really need you, because I have expanded my business in New Zealand as well. Most of the time I have to be in New Zealand, and you could help me out in Fiji." Mahesh's manager thought that Mahesh has returned to Fiji forever.

When he learnt that Mahesh is here just for a holiday, he said to Mahesh "I will pay you the same amount of money you getting in Canada, plus I have a vacant house where you can stay." Mahesh thought he was joking. His friend was not kidding, he needed Mahesh. Mahesh explained to him that he is not a Canadian citizen yet. He should get his Canadian Citizens in the next two to three years, at that time he can come and stay in Fiji as a consultant, and work for him. Mahesh's kids told him that there was no way that they would come back to Fiji to live. Only for holidays. Mahesh told his kids they did not have to come, he will come by himself.

Stop-over in California

After the vacation, it was time to return to Canada. This was the hardest part, saying goodbye to their family. Their families and some of the relatives came to drop them off at the airport. They hired a bus to come to the airport. All of the families and friends were very sad and wondering when will the next visit be. While checking in the luggage when they were going through security, his parents and families were just looking at them. They hugged the kids very tightly so many times. There was tears in his mom's eyes, and his dad pretending like everything was normal. Mahesh knew is dad was very sad but did not want to say anything. Finally, they said goodbye to Mahesh and his family and returned to Tailevu. After boarding on to the plane Mahesh had a sick feeling in his stomach, and just wanted to run back. At that moment, he didn't care about his dream and future in Canada. But Mahesh knew, once he gets his Canadian Citizenship, he can bring his parents to Canada. His little son was crying also, when asked what happened, he replied he was missing his grandfather and grandmother. Everyone started crying. Mahesh said to his son not to worry, because we will bring grandfather and grandmother to Toronto very soon, and they will stay with us. Mahesh's wife and kids became normal after they landed in California, United State of America. From the airport, they hired a taxi and went to Bijma's sister's house.

His kids enjoyed San Francisco. They went to see the Golden Bridge during the night. And in the day time they went on a boat ride to Alcatraz Island. It is said this is the first lighthouse United States built. There was a history around three prisoners who escaped from this island. And the kids enjoyed driving through downtown hills. After spending two days in California at Bijma's sister's house, they flew back to Toronto. Mahesh got busy again like before, because he needed to pay the bank loan. The bank loan did not take long to payoff, because there were four adults living in one house. All the expenses were divided amongst them.

Mahesh's Parents
Visit Canada

ahesh's three brothers migrated overseas, two in Australia and one in New Zealand. They always sent some money home, so their parents could retire. Eventually his parents did retire and decided to visit their kids in Canada.

Mahesh's parents went to Vancouver, BC. They stayed at Bro's house, for their granddaughter's wedding. This was the same cousin who was an assistant manager at Industrial Marine Engineering Limited. Mahesh and his wife went to Vancouver to meet them, and after the wedding, Mahesh asked his parents to come to Toronto. But his oldest cousin residing in Edmonton, Alberta, wanted them to come to his house first.

Mahesh's parents went to Edmonton first and then Toronto. Mahesh paid return airfare to bring them to Toronto. Mahesh's parents liked Toronto very much because Buddy and his family was living with him, as well as his nephew, Ramon. Ramon was Bijma's sister's son, and was in his 20s. Ramon stayed home most of the time and took Mahesh's parents out for rides. Sometimes he would take them to taste wine.

Mahesh's parents were very happy in Toronto. They liked how there were so many people living in one house. Mahesh bought a used car, a four-door Honda Accord. One of the features of this car is that the headlights are hidden. You would need to turn on the engine on to see them. Mahesh showed his car to his parents and said, "Dad, you cannot drive this car at night, because there are no headlights." His father replied, "Please return the car right away." Mahesh laughed and showed them the headlights. Mahesh's father wanted to drive, but Mahesh did not allow him, because in Canada we drive on right hand side and in Fiji they drove on left side. Mahesh's father and mother were very much attached with their grandkids and with Buddy's children. Most of the time, Mahesh's father would go downstairs in the basement where Buddy lived with his family and spent time with them, because he stayed home during the daytime.

Mahesh's father always told his mother that whenever he passed away, that she could stay in Toronto, because he knew that she would like living there better than anywhere else. One day his eldest cousin from Edmonton called and said to Mahesh he wanted them back in Edmonton again. Mahesh could not say no to him, because he was the eldest in their family.

After spending six weeks in Toronto, they went back to Edmonton, and then back to Fiji. This time they were not very sad because they spent a lot of time with Mahesh and his kids, and they wanted Mahesh to sponsor them in the near future. Mahesh said he will sponsor very them soon and they could come to Canada to live with him forever.

However, before Mahesh could sponsor his parents, he got a call from Fiji that his father was not feeling well. Within one year's time his father got very sick. Mahesh went to Fiji again and stayed there for more than two weeks, until his dad got a little better. His father was showing progress after 2 weeks. Therefore, Mahesh decided to return to Toronto.

Trouble at the Border

Ramon was living in Canada under refugee status, while waiting for permanent residency in Canada. His family lived in Modesto, California. Ramon's sister was getting married and he wanted to attend her wedding. One day he asked Mahesh to drive him to the US border, in Niagara Falls. Ramon did not see his sister for very long time. Mahesh asked his nephew, "How will you cross the border without a Visa?" Ramon said that he had checked with immigration, and the documents he had were good to cross the border. Mahesh decided to drive him through the Niagara Falls border to the Buffalo airport. Mahesh's nephew had his flight from Buffalo, because the airfare was cheaper than flying from Toronto Pearson International airport.

When they arrived at the border when the officer asked for the passport. Mahesh handed over his, then the officer asked for his nephew's documents. Ramon replied they are with the passport handed over to the border officer. When the officer checked the documents, his nephew became under suspicion. Ramon had his brother's green card in Mahesh's passport. The officer knew there was something fishy and told them to park their car on the side and come with him in the office. The officer said to Mahesh and his nephew in a stern voice, "You two are in very big trouble, and could go to jail for five years."

The border officer handed the documents to his senior officer. Mahesh was very scared, and worried about his future. He had a mortgage on the house, plus his daughter was in college. The senior officer asked them why they were crossing the border without proper documents. Mahesh explained that his nephew's sister was getting married, and he wanted to attend the wedding. He explained his nephew did not see his sister for long time. Mahesh told the officer that before we left home that he did ask his nephew if he had the proper documents to cross the border, and his nephew replied yes. Mahesh's nephew confirmed what Mahesh told the officer. Mahesh told them that he had no idea that his nephew placed his brother's green card in Mahesh's passport.

Ramon admitted that he did it when Mahesh went to fill gas in his car. The officer told them that they both had to go back to Canada. It was big relief when the officer said to them, "Crossing the border is not a crime," and that they could not be sent to jail for it. However, they would have to come back with their lawyer to court and tell the judge exactly what they said to the officer. The officer then said to Mahesh "Please take everything out of your car." Mahesh was shocked, and asked "Officer sir I do not understand?" The officer replied, "Since your nephew's green card was in your passport, and you handed it over to the border officer we will have to seize your car. You can claim it the same day you when you come to court."

Mahesh and his nephew were so happy that they were not sent to jail. Mahesh was never scared like this in his life before. This was his first offence, and this is not who he is. Mahesh went to his lawyer to fight for his case. His lawyer said he could not fight his case in United States of America, Mahesh had to find one in the US. His lawyer told him not to worry because it is not an offence to cross the border. Just attend court and tell the judge what happened on that day.

Mahesh and Ramon went to court and told the judge exactly what happened. How his nephew wanted to attend his sister's wedding, and Mahesh had no idea when he inserted his brother's green card in his passport. The judge did not fine them but banned them from entering United State of America for one year. The judge told Mahesh to take his car, and just pay for the storage fees. Mahesh claimed his car and paid the storage fees. The storage fee was more than the cost of his car, but Mahesh did not want to leave his car behind.

Hans Raj

Mahesh and Bijma were working very hard to cover all the expenses of maintaining their house. Due to his hard work and good service for ten years, he qualified for a trip to Beijing, China. This prize was a manager's incentive. Managers were giving tickets to their employees from Toronto to China. Then Mahesh got a call that his father was very sick again. Mahesh went to his manager and asked if he could change the ticket from China to Fiji. His manager was very nice to him and gave Mahesh a cheque for the same amount, allowing Mahesh to go to Fiji to see his father. He was there for three weeks and by his father's side most of the time.

When he was coming back to Canada, his father was very sad. Mahesh's father was probably thinking that it might be the last time he will be seeing his son. He held Mahesh very tightly for one minute and said goodbye with tears in his eyes.

His father was right. Mahesh's father passed away within one month. Mahesh was not able to go back to Fiji and attend his father's funeral. His expenses were too high, and he just could not afford it. He was so distressed and angry inside. He did not show his emotions because he did not want his wife and kids to worry about him.

One day, Buddy came with a video tape that Mahesh's father recorded when he was in Toronto. Mahesh did not know about this video tape. Mahesh's father left the video tape with his brother-in-law Buddy and gave strict instructions to give the tape to Mahesh after his death. Mahesh was shocked, overwhelmed and excited to watch the recording. In the video tape, his father advised Mahesh that he did not have to come for his funeral, as it would be very expensive. His only request was for Mahesh to try to bring his mom to Toronto to stay with them, and to take care of her. He told Mahesh that she would like to stay with Mahesh and his wife. This video tape was a big relief for Mahesh. He did not feel guilty for not attending his father's funeral anymore. He knew his father was very understanding and caring. Mahesh felt so much better.

One year later, all of his brothers and sisters wanted him to come to Fiji for their father's prayer. In the Hindu religion the final prayer and reunion is to be done one year after a person's death. Everyone was there, and his mom wanted to see him, as Mahesh is the eldest son. Because he is the eldest in the family, he had to be there. Mahesh borrowed some money from family and friends and went to Fiji again to attend the ceremony and to see his family.

Sumintra Devi

Shortly after coming back from his father's prayer, Mahesh was determined to help his mother come and live with them for her remaining years. Unfortunately, this was going to be very hard, as he received a call that she was not well.

Mahesh went to Fiji by himself for two weeks to see his mother. Mahesh could not afford to take his wife or stay longer than two weeks in Fiji. All his brothers and sisters were there waiting for him. Mahesh's mom was admitted into the hospital. Mahesh went every day to the hospital and stayed with his mom all day. Mahesh's younger brother, Jovan, is a pharmacist. He resides in Sydney, Australia. He also came to Fiji to see their mom. He would always consult with the doctors about his mother's health. One day, he came back from consulting with the doctors and told everyone that their mom had cancer, and it passed stage one. It was very difficult to get treatment in Fiji.

Everyone was very sad, especially Mahesh, because he had to leave to go back to Canada. Mahesh did not know what to do. It was not affordable to stay longer in Fiji and he could not tell his mom that he had to return to Canada soon. Mahesh and his brothers decided not to tell their mom that she has cancer, probably mom would not understand what cancer even was. Those days they did not understand about life insurance or critical illness insurance, so it was not affordable to take overseas for treatment.

They did not tell their mom anything about her illness. One day when she was feeling a little better, she asked Mahesh, "When are you going back to Canada?" She said to Mahesh, "You should go back. I am getting better." Mahesh had two more days to stay in Fiji, but he did not say anything to his mom. After one day, Mahesh told his mother he would return to Canada when she feels better. Mahesh was staying in the hospital all the time. Most of the time sitting on the floor without eating, and sleeping, sometimes he would just cry. He wanted to help and make his mom feel better, but he could not do anything. He felt useless. Finally, he told his mom he had to go back to Canada, but he will come and see her again next year.

He flew back to Toronto the next day. After two weeks, Mahesh got a call from his brother that she passed away. Mahesh and his wife could not afford to attend the funeral. This was the second time Mahesh and Bijma could not afford to attend a funeral for someone they cared about.

Buying a New House

After a few years in this house, Mahesh's kids are grown and they needed more space. The family needed a bigger house, with separate bedrooms for 3 of his kids to study for their exams and for them to have their own personal space. One day, Mahesh and his wife were driving in the neighborhood and saw an advertisement for new houses coming soon. Mahesh and his wife went into the office and collected some brochures and price lists. Mahesh found some semi-detached houses at an affordable price. Mahesh discussed with Buddy, and they decided to purchase one property as well. Semi-detached, side-by-side each other. The builder agreed to take a small deposit because the construction will be complete after one year. Mahesh and Buddy had lot of time to save up money for the down payment. Mahesh and his brother-in-law listed their house for sale. Within one month their house was sold. The buyer wanted to close the deal in sixty days. Mahesh's agent advised them to close the deal, because they were getting a good price for their property. They can rent some place for eight months and move when his house was ready. They both agreed and accepted the offer.

After the closing, they needed to rent a property until the construction for the new house was completed. They needed a place to stay right away for eight months. They found one house in a different city with high rent. They had no choice but to rent it for eight months. Mahesh saw the landlord had a sign for sale on that property also, so he took this opportunity to not make any contracts with the landlord. The landlord wanted a one-year contract. Mahesh said to him if he manages to sell this property, we will move out. You do not have to give us any notice. Mahesh also mentioned that they had bought a house, it will be ready after one year. The landlord was a nice person, he did not take any deposit. And the landlord did not say anything when they moved into their new house after eight months. When they moved into their new house, everyone felt very happy and relaxed. The kids enjoyed their space and were friendlier with each other. It seemed like Mahesh's dreams were coming true. As you know, Mahesh has big dreams, to have his own house, SUV in the garage, private office on top floor of glass building.

Soon after buying their new house, Kitty decided to get married and move out. Although this seemed like it was moving quickly, and Mahesh was not completely financially prepared to host people at his home for the wedding, he quickly made the necessary arrangements and did whatever he could. Mahesh could not ask them to postpone the wedding, as the hall was booked and paid for. In addition, some of his cousins from Los Angeles and Vancouver had already arranged to attend the wedding. His cousin, Bro was coming from Vancouver and his cousin Master, was coming from Los Angeles. The wedding and reception went smoothly, and everyone had a great time.

Financial Troubles

After the wedding Mahesh found out that someone had been using his credit cards, since back from when he was in Fiji. The purchases were made in a store that he had never been to or heard of before.

When he realized this, he started investigating. The bank found out that all of his credit cards were compromised. Some of the credit card companies refused to pay or investigate. Only one bank agreed to refund the entire amount under one condition, which was that he had to close all the other accounts. The bank manager told him that the bank would pay all his credit cards and the bank would give him one credit card to use for emergency purposes, but the interest rate was high. The interest rate could be reduced in the future once his credit rating improved. The credit limit was only $5,000. Mahesh did not have any other options, he accepted the condition and accepted the credit card with the high interest rate. Mahesh consolidated all the credit cards, and just kept one for emergency use.

Sometimes Mahesh would get frustrated and upset when he did not have enough money, and if things were not going well for him. One day he went to the bank and was standing in line for more than twenty minutes. When he reached the bank teller, she told Mahesh that he had to go to the cashier at the end of the counter. Mahesh went to that lady cashier at the end of the counter. The lady cashier said to him, "You have to go wait in the line." Mahesh explained to her that he was already in the line, even some customers confirmed he was standing in the line. She did not listen to anyone and said "I saw him coming directly to me." Mahesh went back in the line and went to the same teller. In a stern voice, Mahesh said, "Close my account, and give me all my money". The teller was shocked. She responded, "What?" Mahesh got frustrated and asked her, "Do you understand English?" and repeated, "Please close my account, and give me my money".

The bank teller asked, "Why do you want to close your account?" Mahesh responded, "Does it matter?" Teller answered in a snooty tone, "Yes it does matter. I need to write a report." Mahesh replied very loudly, "I do not like your attitude. You are rude and do not want to help me." The Bank manager came out from his office due to the commotion and asked what happened. Mahesh explained to him how the bank teller and the cashier treated him. And how he was not happy with the service. The manager apologized to Mahesh and went back into his office. The teller asked Mahesh again "What can I do for you?" Mahesh was getting frustrated and out of anger replied, "Close my account. I have told you so many times. Or do you want me to come inside and do it for you? Or do I have to call police for this? Then will you close my account, and give me my money?" The bank manager came out again, and told the cashier to go in his office, and he sent another cashier to help Mahesh. Mahesh was very upset because this bank's credit card was also compromised, and they didn't do anything to help him.

Mahesh's expenses were more than his income. He became depressed and didn't know what to do. His daughter and son-in-law advised him to sell his house and stay with them until everything became under control. Mahesh and his wife sold the house, and they moved in with his daughter Kitty. Poonam and Vishal also moved in with Kitty. Mahesh managed to pay off his credit card, as well as the money he borrowed from relatives and friends. As soon as everything was paid off, Mahesh had another challenge, his second daughter wanted to get married. She just completed college, and she did not want to go for further education, because she started working at a Bank.

Poonam's Wedding

In 2005, Mahesh's second daughter, Poonam, found a boy named Dhruv who she wanted to marry. He and his family were from India. They have a very big family in India and Canada. Their relatives from India also wanted to come for the wedding. Mahesh's daughter also wanted a nice religious ceremony, and reception, with all her friends. She wanted all of her family to come to her wedding. Some of Mahesh's brothers, sisters and cousins, also wanted to attend the wedding. This was going to be a very big wedding, and Mahesh knew he would have to save a lot of money to help his daughter pay for it.

Luckily, the wedding had to be postponed for six months, which gave Mahesh some more time to save money. Poonam had also found a job, and Vishal started working as a salesman in a retail store. This all helped with covering expenses at home and for the wedding.

After six months, it was time for Poonam's wedding celebrations. Visitors from overseas liked the wedding. Mahesh arranged hotels for his family to stay in during the wedding. Guests were coming from Fiji, Australia, the United States of America, Edmonton and Vancouver. There wasn't enough space for everyone to stay at Kitty's house, so Mahesh booked hotels for some of the visitors.

Mahesh was happy to take them to the CN Tower, Rogers Centre, Casa Loma, Toronto Island, Wonderland, and Niagara Falls. Their favorite place was Niagara Falls because Mahesh took them on the journey behind the falls tour. He also took them on a boat tour in Niagara Gorge to the foot of the falls. Although Mahesh was trying not to use his credit cards, he didn't really have a choice, and used them to ensure his family had a good time, and his daughter had the wedding she wanted.

In the end it was all worth it. There was a nice wedding and reception with help from all family members. Visitors from abroad said that it was one of the best wedding and reception they've been to. All those who visited from overseas loved spending time in Toronto.

Spending time with his family made Mahesh happy. This was the happiest he's been in a very long time.

The last time he was this happy was when his first grandson, Lucian, was born. He and Buddy finished a full bottle of whisky in celebration. The one his son-in-law Navin, the new father, kept for a long time as a souvenir. Since he was a new father, he probably wasn't going to drink it anyway.

Moving out of Kitty's House

A round 2 years after Lucian was born, Kitty and Navin had a second baby. Everything was moving nicely. Because Kitty's family was growing, Mahesh, his wife and Vishal decided to buy their own house and to move out from Kitty's house. Vishal also wanted to help them to buy their own property as soon as possible. So, they started looking for houses close to Kitty's house.

One day Mahesh and Bijma were driving in a nice neighborhood, close to the lake, and saw a sign for new houses that were coming soon. They went in to the office to inquire about the price, and when the house will be built. The agent told him it will be ready in the following year.

After reviewing all the options, they decided to buy one of those properties. One that would be suitable for his family. They picked a single-family house, with three floors. Three floors so Vishal can have his own floor and some personal space. Because the new house wouldn't be built for a year, they had some time to save some money and make the down payments.

Mahesh gave the agent the deposit to hold the property they wanted. His son liked the house because he had the top floor by himself, and the house was walking distance from the lake in a quiet neighbourhood. Mahesh felt lucky, his dreams were back on track and coming true again, Mahesh and Bijma started working very hard. Vishal also worked part time, and after one year, they moved into their new house.

Sun Life Financial

After a few years at the new house, Vishal decided that he wanted to go back to school and pursue further education as a full-time student. Because of this, it was very difficult for them to pay the mortgage and other expenses without his son's income. Vishal understood all this, but he also wanted to further his education, as he was just working in a retail store at the time. Mahesh understood how important education is and encouraged Vishal to go back to college.

Although it would be hard on them financially, Mahesh wanted to keep the property and not have to sell it. Mahesh and Bijma made some lifestyle adjustments and started working on cutting unnecessary expenses. They only purchased what was needed, and stopped going out of Toronto for vacations. They also decided to stop playing slot machines at the casino, which took a lot of self-control as this was a hobby of theirs.

It was very hard to manage the property, but he did not want to sell this property. Mahesh also did not want to go back into debt. He wanted to be in control of his life. He had big dreams to accomplish, but sometimes he felt like he was stuck in a loop. Mahesh knew that his current job wasn't going to lead him to his dream.

One day, Mahesh and his wife were driving passed his wife's brother's house and decided to stop by and see what his brother-in-law was doing. Mahesh saw a nice lady in the kitchen table talking to them. His brother-in-law introduced her to them; she was from Sun Life Financial, and they were planning to get life insurance for themselves. Mahesh and Bijma decided to leave them alone while they discussed this with the lady but told he his brother-in-law to go for it. Sun Life Financial is one of the biggest and the most recognized companies in Canada.

From that day forward that insurance agent kept calling Mahesh, trying to get him to join them as an advisor at Sun Life. This insurance agent had been employed there for more than five years. She knew that Mahesh had a life insurance licence, which he obtained two years before. But since this type of work is commission-based, Mahesh could not afford to go on contract with any insurance brokerages, his expenses were a little high. He could not afford to quit his job at that time. Mahesh's brother-in-law told the lady that Mahesh has a life insurance licence, but he was not able to work as an insurance agent at the time.

The insurance agent explained to Mahesh how Sun Life Financial company was different and how it worked. She went over the commission, and advanced payment option. She explained to Mahesh that he will receive some money in advance. She encouraged Mahesh to meet with her manager and he will be able to better explain everything to him. This woman knew Mahesh had potential and she knew he would be an asset to the company. She further explained how this company treats their advisors, and she said the company will deposit six thousand dollars in advance to your reserve account. If your commission is not more than a thousand dollars in any paycheque, they used this money, so your pay will be more than a thousand dollars, and after three years whatever is leftover will be deposited to your bank account. Mahesh did not refuse her, but he said to her that he would think about it. The insurance agent advised Mahesh, she knows he has big dreams, but sometimes you have to take risks for those dreams.

The Sun Life insurance advisor started calling him every day again once he returned from Fiji. She wanted Mahesh to meet with her manager. Mahesh was so confused and undecided. He did not want to quit his job from Canada Post. But then he started noticing how the staff from Canada Post would park their car in their own parking spots every day and came in whenever they wanted. They made their own schedule. They had flexibility. This was Mahesh's dream. He wanted his own office and his own schedule.

Mahesh thought maybe Sun Life Financial was his future. The Canada Post job was only contract based, which he had to renew every five years. If they don't renew the next five-year contract, Mahesh would be out of a job anyway, and he would also miss this Sun Life opportunity. Sun Life Financial seemed like the right decision for his goals. He could just see his own office, schedule and parking spot.

Mahesh decided to join the Sun Life Insurance Company and went to see the agent's manager for more information. The manager explained how Sun Life Financial does business. The manager told Mahesh that he would be challenged and inspired to do his best every day. He told Mahesh that he would be surrounded by people who recognize his potential and encourage him to flourish. He'll be rewarded for his contributions as an individual and as a group. He told Mahesh that they're always looking for outstanding people.

The manager also mentioned that the manager's duty is to help all the advisors build their financial future, and live a brighter, healthier life. The manager said, "Reader's Digest rated Sun Life Financial as the number one insurance company in Canada. Mahesh, as an advisor, your duty is to educate the client about their future. Help your clients to reach their financial goal. Teach your clients how to start a budget, and grow their savings in a tax smart investment. Your goal is to help them find insurance products to meet their requirements within their budget."

Mahesh didn't know how he would be able to do all this, or if he was even capable. Mahesh's face showed his fear, and the manager noticed. The manager looked at Mahesh, and said, "Don't worry. You will have full training, and this is like your own business. You will be self-employed under the Sun Life Financial Company." The manager advised, "In the beginning it is a little difficult, but once you build your business everything will be manageable. We are here to help until you become fully confident. Plus, you will get an advance for $6000, which you do not have to return".

Mahesh liked the idea of moving into the commission-based role at Sun Life and gave the Canada Post position a four-week notice. Mahesh took his first step with Sun Life and joined one of the biggest insurance companies in Canada for training. In the beginning it was difficult just as the manager said, but in short time with hard work and helpful people, Mahesh had become a Sun Life advisor.

Because of Mahesh's educational background, he struggled a lot. But he would never miss any training sessions or seminars. Mahesh was very committed to learning as much as he can to be a very successful advisor. Mahesh paid eight hundred dollars to attend the World Critical Illness Insurance seminar held in Toronto by Dr Marius Barnard. Dr. Marius Barnard is a renowned heart surgeon. And there were so many top speakers from all over the world. There were speakers from Australia, England, and from other countries. Mahesh learned that in year 1983, critical illness insurance was founded by Dr Barnard. He recognized the financial plight of his patients who survived a critical illness and could not afford the medication.

Dr. Barnard was a heart surgeon in South Africa. During his speech he mentioned the good news is that with advancements in medical science, more and more people are surviving critical illnesses. Therefore, it has become increasingly more important to consider the financial hardship that may occur if you were ever faced with a critical illness in your lifetime. Dr. Barnard mentioned that 50,000 Canadians suffer a stroke each year and 75% survive their first stroke, but without insurance it is very difficult to survive.

Mahesh also attended Mr. Brian Tracy's seminar. His speech was called "Achieve Your Goals -Fast". The cost included ten CD's regarding achievements and The Power of Habit. Mr. Tracy is an international speaker. Mahesh was so motivated after attending his seminars, but he did not listen to all his speeches because he thought Mr. Tracy's CDs can be listened to afterwards. One day one of his colleagues asked to borrow those CDs for a week, and she promised that she would return them in one week. But she did not return the

CDs. She quit Sun Life and disappeared. She did not answer any of Mahesh's phone calls or emails.

Mahesh learned that there are over fifty life insurance companies in Canada. Building financial security later in life is difficult, especially while people are looking towards retirement. Apparently, life insurance is increasingly becoming the tool that Canadians are using to protect their retirement. After attending all the seminars Mahesh had learned a lot of different techniques on how to help clients. He liked the umbrella theory - better to have it and not need it, then to need it and not have it.

The theory is this; if you carry an umbrella, there won't be rain. This was something like what Mahesh's father used to say to him. Basically, always be prepared. The theory applies not just to rain, but to the managing of your life. The idea is to give prior thought to what might happen and prepare for it.

Finding Success

Mahesh was always dedicated to the work he was doing for his clients. He was very helpful to his clients and was becoming a very successful advisor. He managed to earn most campaign and manager incentives. This was new to Mahesh, as a lot of the incentives had to do with travel, and they were usually to places Mahesh had never been to.

The first incentive he earned was a trip to Eastern Ontario. Winners of the incentive took a chartered bus to the city of Ottawa, the capital of Canada. This was the first time Mahesh went to Ottawa. They spent more than three hours there. Everyone went to the Parliament House on Parliament Hill. It is an area of crown land on the south side of the Ottawa River in downtown Ottawa. When they went inside, the tour guide asked the group, "Do you know why the chairs are green?" Mahesh quickly replied, "Because they're made in Pakistan?" Everyone started to laugh.

After the Parliament House they went to the flower garden, and then to see where precious coins were made. They got to hold gold bars in their hands. The gold bars were locked in chains and two policemen were guarding them with loaded guns. After lunch, the next stop was in Montreal. They went in the church to light the candles. It was a very big church on the top of the hill, it was a very nice location, but you had to climb almost three hundred steps to get in the church. In the church you can see a lot of walking canes. They say most of the people came here with a cane and did not need them after lighting the candle. The name of the church is Saint Joseph's Oratory of Mount Royal, which is the most famous church in Montreal.

After lighting the candles, they went to a museum to see all kinds of birds and animals. It was at this museum where Mahesh saw the most disgusting thing he's ever seen in his life. It was a huge rat that was the size of a pig.

The last stop was Quebec City, the capital of the province of Quebec. They spent the night in a five-star hotel. It was an elegant hotel. The food was delicious. The next day, very early in the morning, they went to the top of the hill to see the sunrise. The tour guide said that this is the best scene in the world, to see the sunrise. Mahesh said to everyone, that the tour guide never been to Fiji Islands.

After this trip Mahesh became more motivated and wanted to qualify for all the campaigns. Sun Life Financial has three major campaigns every year. Mahesh wanted to study for the mutual fund exam as well, but the mutual fund exam was not easy. Mahesh knew he can make more commission from investing clients' money, which would make it easier to qualify for campaigns. However, the course was not easy. Mahesh studied very hard to obtain mutual fund licence. He failed three times. But finally, on his fourth attempt he passed the exam. He became a financial advisor from an insurance advisor. Mahesh can deal with both mutual funds and insurance clients.

Son's Wedding

Mahesh was starting to make steady money with Sun Life. His business made many improvements.

Vishal wanted to get married and move out to his fiancée, Melissa's condominium that she had for a long time. The wedding ceremony was scheduled for year after their engagement. They found a nice banquet hall called Paradise Banquet Hall. They held the wedding ceremony outside in the garden, with part of the aisle being a Victorian bridge. The weather was so beautiful that day. Everyone enjoyed staying outside in the garden during the wedding ceremony.

The reception was inside the banquet hall. The décor was so elegant and classy. It was so beautiful. During the reception Mahesh's three granddaughters, Anjali, Ria and Chyah performed the opening dance, which everyone liked the most. The girls were between the ages of 5 and 6 at that time. Their mothers, Poonam and Kitty, made them practice for six months to make sure it was perfect. Vishal and his wife couldn't stop smiling. Mahesh and his wife couldn't stop smiling. All of Mahesh's kids found amazing life partners, and he knew their kids spouses will keep his kids happy. That's every father's dream. After the wedding his son moved out of the house, and into his wife's condo.

After all the celebrations were over and his son had moved out, Mahesh and his wife were left with a big five-bedroom house to manage on their own. This was his dream, but keeping up with the costs was not easy for the two of them. Mahesh did not want to sell the house because the location was close to the lake and in a quiet neighbourhood. The value of this property was increasing. Mahesh wanted to keep the house as a place for his grandkids to visit.

In the fall, some of Mahesh's colleagues came to celebrate the Diwali festival at his house. They enjoyed it very much. The party lasted until after midnight. Lots of singing, dancing, and drinking. Some of his friends advised him not to sell the house. They said it is a very nice house, and it is in a good neighborhood. Mahesh and Bijma were having a very hard time again but did not want to sell the house. They did not want to sell the house because it was in a good location, and he felt like it would be a shame for them to sell the property in such a short time. He just could not bear the thought of selling this home.

Importance of building trust and friendships

One day one of Mahesh's female colleagues called him to her residence to talk about business. When Mahesh went to meet her, she was not well. She could not get out of bed, and was in a sedated state. She told Mahesh that she was really sick and needed his help. Her plan was to transfer all her clients to his block of business. She told him that she liked working with him but cannot come to the office. She wanted Mahesh to take over her office. It was bigger than Mahesh's. She told Mahesh that her office is on the thirteenth floor, with glass windows. It had a nice view of downtown, and she had new furniture which he would just have to pay half price for. Mahesh told her that he was willing to help but felt guilty about taking all her clients.

He told her that he can move into her office for now and pay for the furniture, and when she got better than they could work together. Mahesh also told her that she can stay home, and he would take care of all her appointments. And as soon as she gets better, they both can use the office. Mahesh told her that they can do business "jointly". Mahesh asked his colleague, "What exactly happened to you? What did the doctors say? And what made you pick me?" Mahesh didn't understand why she would choose him, when she had a good female friends in the office.

She replied to Mahesh, "You are the most trustworthy, and honest person I ever met". She asked Mahesh to help her. The doctors were doing all kinds of tests, and she did not know when she would get better. The doctors were not telling her what exactly happened to her. She had heartburn that was getting worse every day. She pleaded again to Mahesh to help her. Mahesh reassured her that she will get better soon because she is still young and healthy. When she gets better, Mahesh will reconsider her offer. She insisted Mahesh to take the offer, but Mahesh is not a greedy man, he would always help people with no strings attached.

Mahesh finally agreed to help her. He took-over her office and paid for the furniture. She just bought new furniture from the firm. In this company all the advisors had to pay for the office space because they are self-employed and on commission. Now Mahesh has to pay more money for the office, but it was a big office on the thirteenth floor, with glass windows and a nice view of downtown Toronto.

This was his dream, his own office, his own spot to park his car, and his own time to come in the office. Mahesh could not believe how trusted he was. It seemed like he had achieved his goal. This was his dream. This is the dream Mahesh had been chasing his whole life. After one week, Mahesh's colleague's husband called, and told him that his wife passed away. Her funeral was the next day at 2pm. It was a Saturday evening, Mahesh was drinking at Buddy's house when he got the news. He was in shock. He did not know what to do. He quickly called some of his colleagues and informed them. Everything was deadlocked. Mahesh did not have any other option, just to work hard. The manager transferred some of her families and best clients to Mahesh's block of business for service.

Expanding his Business

Mahesh's expenses were becoming more than his income. He needed to sign more clients, so he decided to take the mutual funds licence and life insurance licence exams for another province. Mahesh has three cousins in Edmonton, one in Calgary, and one in Vancouver. Mahesh's wife has two brothers in Edmonton. Mahesh called his nephew, his oldest cousin's son who is a CEO of Structural Steel Company in Edmonton. His nephew convinced Mahesh to come to Edmonton and they will support him to boost his business. So, Mahesh started studying hard to get his Alberta Life Insurance Licence and within three months' time he obtained both licences. Passing the exam for mutual fund licence was very tough for him but he did not give up. After failing a few times, he obtained his licence and was able to conduct business in Alberta.

Whenever Mahesh went to Edmonton for business, he did not have to stay in a hotel or rent a car. His nephew always gave him his car to use, and he stayed at his eldest cousin's residence. Mahesh did not have to pay for food, transport or hotel. He just had to pay for airfare. Since his nephew was a CEO in Structural Steel company, he got the best car with a full tank of gas. Mahesh got a lot of business from him as well. Because Mahesh had licences for two provinces, Alberta and Ontario, his business started growing faster and he qualified for most of the campaigns, and managers incentives every year.

Mahesh enjoyed going to Edmonton, he always found something to do. He liked going to the West Edmonton mall if he did not have any appointments, as they have casino and Mahesh liked to play slot machines.

Finding more Successes at Sun Life

Mahesh was finding a lot of success getting clients and making sales when in Edmonton. He was doing so well that he qualified for a two-night stay at Blue Mountain, an alpine ski resort two hours from Toronto. It was very close to a clear water lake called Northwinds beach. There was nice weather, so most of time Mahesh and Bijma went swimming with some of his colleagues, which he enjoyed very much. The food was delicious and there was a lot of entertainment in the evening. Everyone had a great time.

Within four months, there was another campaign, and Mahesh won a two-night stay at the Muskoka Resort, north of Toronto. It took three hours to drive there. Muskoka is considered one of the best places to visit in Canada. Mahesh was able to do a number of exciting things that he would never have known to do before.

Australia Wedding

One day, Mahesh's brother, Nawal, called and invited him to his son's wedding in Sydney, Australia. The wedding was within eight months and his brother wanted him to come. All of his brothers and sisters were planning to be at this wedding. Mahesh's brother had three kids, and all three were getting married at the same time.

Mahesh and Bijma decided to attend this wedding and visit his uncle and aunty (Mahesh's father's sister) who lived in Brisbane, Australia. They are over ninety years old. The last time Mahesh saw them was when they were in Fiji, more than twenty-five years ago. Mahesh's financial situation was not very good, but since Bijma was employed full time and could afford to help with the expenses, they decided to go.

Mahesh's nephew was the first to get married. It ended up that only this nephew got married, the other two weddings had been postponed. However, it was a very nice wedding. The night after the wedding was the remembrance night. For most of the family it was their first time together after many years. Mahesh made a speech. During his speech, he asked everyone who should be credited for them being there that day. There was a lot of thoughts on who should be credited and most of them answered that his brother for inviting everyone. Mahesh told them they were all wrong. Today they were all there because of his father. He remembered when Tom Edward asked his dad to take over the island job. Mahesh was so happy, but his dad refused. His father wanted them to be civilized, not to become "bahilla". If his father took the island job they wouldn't be there today. Everyone agreed. After the wedding, they went to visit their uncle and aunty in Brisbane. Mahesh's uncle and aunty were very happy to see them. Even though, Mahesh's uncle and aunty were in their nineties, they were still strong. One night one of Mahesh's cousins took them to the casino to play the slots. His cousin also likes to play slots at the casino.

Trip to Las Vegas

After his vacation Mahesh started working harder, doing business in Ontario and Alberta, which helped him qualify for another campaign. This time it was a one-week trip to Las Vegas.

It was a dream of Mahesh to visit Las Vegas for a long time. He was so excited to be in Las Vegas to play the slot machines. Mahesh asked his two cousins to join him in Las Vegas. His cousin from Vancouver came with his wife. His cousin Master, who was living in Los Angeles, also came with his wife. It was a great opportunity for them to meet up and have fun.

His hotel was booked by his company in the heart of Las Vegas, the MGM Grand. Every street you walked on, you can see a casino, even in the airport they had slot machines. There were lots of things to see and do. Mahesh and his family rented a van and drove to Grand Canyon National Park in Arizona, about a six-hour drive from Las Vegas. The next morning Mahesh and his family visited the Hoover

Dam. One week went by very fast. Mahesh had spent a lot of money, but he also had many good times with his cousins.

**Mahesh and Master with their
spouses at the Grand Canyon.**

Atlantic City

If you walk into Mahesh's office, you will see a lot of trophies and awards. He was getting very good at his job and usually qualified for trophies, campaigns and awards. One time he qualified for a four-day bus trip to Atlantic City, New Jersey, in the US. Atlantic City is a resort city. The slot machines were two steps away from his room. On the last day in the early morning, Bijma was playing a one-cent slot machine. She kept getting free spins. It felt like over a hundred times. The machine kept giving more spins.

All the while, everyone was on the bus waiting for them, so they can leave for Toronto. But Mahesh and his wife couldn't leave the machine until it stopped the free spins. Finally, the machine stopped, and the attendant paid the jackpot money. Everyone thought they were lost in the hotel. After waiting for about an hour, they saw Mahesh and Bijma laughing and shouting "JACKPOT! JACKPOT!" Mahesh told everyone on the bus why they were late. Bijma won the jackpot on the one-penny machine. It took them one full day to drive back to Toronto.

One pill, two pill, three pill, four.

Mahesh used all kinds of techniques to improve his business, like distributing flyers and hiring telemarketers from India to book appointments for him. In the beginning it worked nicely but most of the time they did not book genuine appointments, so he decided not to continue. Mahesh started to book his own appointments himself. In this business, it was easy to qualify for campaigns, but it was hard to make a lot of money because of the expenses. He had to pay for office, parking spot, and many more things like gas and phone bills. But he had so many good times in the office and out. His family could also take a vacation with him. In the office, he was liked by his managers and colleagues. He always bought new recruits for the managers. He also helped some of the advisors, if they needed it. Mostly to drive them to their clients' houses for meetings. He always kept his office door open when he was in. Advisors did not have to knock on his door or set appointments to see him.

Mahesh was very much liked by his friends and families. He was also a member of a small religious club, known as the Hindu Association of Toronto. He always took part in singing and reading Ramayana, the holy book. The Hindu Association of Toronto is a non-profit organization, all the money they collected was for charity. Mahesh was a secretary for more than five years and then in an election he had been elected as vice president. Due to being a member of this religious organization, he became very famous in his committee in Toronto. People knew him as an honest person, which made him more successful in his business.

One day he went to a client's house for a meeting, but his client's wife had to ask Mahesh to come back after two hours because her husband was out. Mahesh went to the nearest restaurant and ate lunch. He only ate vegetarian because he had to do a prayer to read the Ramayana later that day.

Suddenly, he started getting rashes on his face. Mahesh had some allergies to certain types of vegetables and cakes, so he went to the nearest pharmacy and bought a pack of 24-hour allergy relief tablets, and took one tablet right away. He took another one when he got home. Mahesh thought he should take one more before the prayer, so he would feel better when he was there.

When Mahesh was at the prayer, his fever and itchy skin became worse. Mahesh had to go back home. When he got home, he took another tablet and went to bed. His heart started beating faster and he started getting shortness of breath. Mahesh asked his wife to take him to the hospital. When Mahesh got to the front counter, he told the nurse that he must have had an allergic reaction to something he ate and took three or four tablets. He showed the package to the nurse and she quickly called the doctor.

The doctor and nurse took him to a private room and started monitoring everything. He had wires all over his body and machines around his bed. He had one nurse staying with him all the time. After a couple of hours, the doctor checked on him. Mahesh asked the doctor if he can go home since he was feeling better. The doctor told him he had to stay there all night and maybe tomorrow as well. He was given one big glass of charcoal to drink.

Next morning two officers came to ask Mahesh why he wanted to commit suicide. Mahesh started laughing and told the officers exactly what happened. The officers allowed him to go home.

New Orleans

Sun Life had three campaigns every year. Mahesh qualified for another campaign that year. This time it was for a four-day trip to New Orleans. Mahesh and Bijma drove from Toronto to Buffalo, New York. The plan was to drive with one of his colleagues and his wife to Buffalo, to save money on airplane tickets. Sun Life had paid their advisors to arrange their own air tickets. His colleague dropped out at the very end. His colleague did not qualify because some of his clients cancelled their insurance policies. Mahesh and his wife drove themselves to the Buffalo Airport. They landed in New Orleans by mid-day and arrived in the evening to their hotel. Mahesh didn't know what to do but as soon as he opened his window curtain, he saw a big casino sign on the next street. He told Bijma to look outside; she laughed and said now we have something to do.

After dinner, Mahesh and Bijma went down to cross the street to go to the Casino. The security officer stopped them and asked them where they were going. Mahesh replied they were going to the Casino. The officer told them not to go anywhere without reporting to him first and never to walk down. The security officer called a taxi and took all their information, then allowed them to take the ride. It was only a two-minute drive. Mahesh asked the officer why they would have to take a taxi, since it is only a five-minute walk. The security officer said the two minutes is enough time to get robbed and killed. And on their way back to the hotel, the security officer in the Casino did the same.

Next morning Mahesh and some of his colleagues went to see alligators in a swamp by boat. This boat did not have a propeller, it ran by fan. Mahesh saw huge alligators. He fed them marshmallows and chicken meat. In New Orleans, it was the first time Mahesh saw a cemetery above ground. He was told that a family can buy a plot for a family to use every time a member of their family passes away. There was a lot of nice things to see and do in New Orleans.

The casino was just one block from his hotel. Every night he and Bijma would go to the Casino. And every night, the security officer would stop them. One time there was a different officer and he and his wife tried to sneak by him and walk down. This officer saw them and stopped them. He asked them the same questions before calling a taxi. There was not much time. Four days passed so quickly. Next morning, his flight was back to Buffalo and from Buffalo drive to Toronto. This was the best holiday from his company.

Motivational Speech

Through his dedication to his clients, Mahesh had become a very successful advisor. His determination and passion helped him succeed in anything he did at his branch. One day the financial centre manager asked him to talk about his experience and success at career night. Mahesh agreed to give a speech to new recruits. There were more than twenty candidates in the room. Mahesh opened his speech with an anecdote from when he first came to Canada:

> There are two types of people in this room, just like when a flight lands from overseas, there are two types of passengers. One type of passenger is so scared, worried, checking all the documents a few times before he lands. And after he lands, he asks everyone passing him where to get the luggage, how to get to the immigration and customs desk. Finally, when he gets to the immigration officer, hands over his passport, and landed document to

immigration officer. The officer sends him to custom officer and the custom officer checks all the document. Finally, he is welcomed to Canada. Then he relaxes.

Passenger number two is always relaxed. He enjoys his flight. Once the flight lands, he follows the crowd, collects his luggage, goes through the immigration and customs desk before coming out safely. We have the same procedure in this room. I want all of you to be like passenger number two, relax and to follow your manager or mentor who brought you in this room. They will take all the responsibilities until you become a successful advisor in this business. I am in this Financial company for more than ten years, I have my LLQP. Two years before I joined this company, I was also not sure if this business was best for me or not, like most of you. Just like some of you cannot make any decision, cannot make your mind. I know it is difficult. Just follow your manager, one day you will also become a successful advisor. Today I am regretting that I have lost two years of having my life Insurance licence and not making my mind on the first day. I worked as a salary person. I know what you all are thinking, exactly the same things I was thinking. It is a commission type of income, but it is your business. You have control in your hands. Your manager and mentor are with you all the time to make you a successful advisor. You may be thinking, you have to quit your job. Yes, but you don't have to quit right away. I understand you may be there for a long time and do not want to lose your benefits. You may be thinking, 'where will I get the client?', etc. Let me tell you something, I was with Canada Post full time for more than fifteen years, full coverage, good pay, my office was close to my house. I had the same type of difficulties to make up my mind also. You may be thinking that this is not for me, maybe this works for you but not for me. Yes, you may be right, but how do you know, that you are right, if you do not register, and find out by yourself. If you do not believe me, is good you find out by yourself. If you want to know how deep the swimming pool is, you have to dive right in.

After they listened to Mahesh's speech, most of them signed the very next day.

First Time in Boston

Mahesh was doing well at Sun Life; he qualified for a three-day bus trip to Boston, Massachusetts. The main focus in Boston was to see The Museum of Fine Arts and The New England Aquarium with the giant ocean tank with over 2,000 animals. Boston has the most professional sports and sea foods, red lobster. Mahesh had enjoyed the food and cold beer. The bar they visited was located in a sea port. The most fun was the swan boat ride out in the ocean to watch the dolphins. Mahesh and some of his colleagues bought one day tickets for hop on-hop off bus tour. They went to so many places and ended up in one of the famous harbor landmarks. They had a nice bar on the harbor front. Mahesh liked to watch soccer very much. It was a world cup tournament, so he jumped off the bus, went in the bar, and watched soccer with a cold beer. Next day the bus took them to the old city area. Some of the houses were built in the 1600s.

After this trip, Mahesh became more motivated. Even though he qualified for most of the campaigns, he always helped some of his colleagues, so they can qualify as well.

Mahesh became very upset when one of the managers assigned some of his clients to one of the other advisors. This advisor was his best friend also. As Mahesh always helped everyone, he did not take it seriously, he continued working hard and moving forward.

India

By 2016, Mahesh had four grandkids. Two from his first daughter, a boy and a girl. His second daughter had two girls. Mahesh liked to spend time with his grandchildren. It was more than 10 years, since his second daughter got married. Her in-laws always insisted that Mahesh and Bijma visit India. They came to Mahesh's house and insisted they join them. They told Mahesh and Bijma that this might be their last trip to India. They had planned to go with them for a long time. If Mahesh and Bijma do not accompany them, it would be a very long time before they go again. Mahesh and Bijma decided to take a five-week holiday from work and went to India with his daughter's in-laws.

Mahesh and Bijma arrived in Gujarat, India. They stayed at his daughter's in-laws' home. The first day in Gujarat, they went to the mall to shop. It was a walking distance from where they stayed. The owner of the house, Anko, walked with them to the mall and showed them the road to come back. When they came out from the mall, it was a little dark, and they took a rickshaw motorbike. The richer driver said that he knew the address and the person to where they were going. Mahesh and Bijma jumped in the rickshaw, it was their first rickshaw ride. After riding for a few minutes, Mahesh figured out that this driver was not going in the right direction. Good thing Mahesh had the phone number to where he had to go. Mahesh called Anko and gave the phone to the rickshaw driver and asked him to please talk to this person. The driver and Anko had a small argument, then the rickshaw driver drops them off within a few minutes, to the right address.

Anko was so mad at Mahesh. He kept asking over and over again why did they take the rickshaw, especially after he showed how to come back. Mahesh did not understand why he was so mad. Finally, he asked Mahesh, how much did he pay the driver. Mahesh said only 150 rupees ($1.50 Canadian). Mahesh thought he paid a lot of money, that's why this person is very upset. When he returned to Canada, Anko called Mahesh and explained why he was so angry. He explained to Mahesh that he was very lucky. The rickshaw drivers are not to be trusted. They can rob or kill you for only small amounts of money. He was right. When Mahesh returned to Canada, Bijma and he started watching an Indian TV series on true crime stories in India, Crime Patrol. It was then when they realized how right Anko was. They were really very lucky that they returned home safely.

Next morning, there was a holiday in Gujarat called kite festival. They went to the park on the bank of Sabarmati river. The residence of Mahatma Gandhi was very close to this park. In the park they saw three statues, the first one had his fingers in his ears, and second one have his finger on his lips, and the third one his hand over his eyes. They say this is what Mahatma Gandhi used to say every time, don't see, talk or listen, if it is not honorable.

Gujarat is a holy province of India with lots of Hindu temples. One of the most beautiful temples in Gujarat is Jyotirlingas of Lord Shiva. The story behind this temple is that it was built in gold by the Moon God. Then rebuilt in silver by Ravana. Later, Lord Krishna built it in wood and then King Bhimdev built it in stone.

After the holiday, they hired a tempo (van) with a driver to drive from Gujarat to Goa. It was about a two days drive and the road went through mountains call Khandala. The road was very narrow and they drove in the night. They were so scared. Good thing Mahesh's son-in law's cousin, Akshay, was with them. When they were almost to the top of the hill, there was a hotel, already booked for them to stay for the night. Next morning, they used 4x4 jeep to take them the rest of the way to the top of the mountain. There was a very old temple. They say this temple was built more than two hundred years ago. Built by five brothers from Mahabharat and they believed one of the savior comes in the night and prays in this mandir.

One of the most unforgettable experiences you can have in India is the camel ride. Mahesh and Bijma went on a camel ride. It was easy to climb on the camel, they had a step to climb. But the owner let the camel go by itself. The camel was walking on a cliff. Mahesh called the owner to stop the camel, but no one came. She walked by herself and came to stop at the right spot. This was the scariest part of his trip. Mahesh almost cried when he looked down from the cliff to the bottom of the mountains. Bijma cried the whole time. It is said that if someone fell, no one will look for the body, even the Indian government will not do anything. By the time someone could reach the body, wild animals would have eaten it.

Camel ride in India

The next day they arrived in Goa. It was night, so they went straight in the hotel and rested. They had driven through the highway with no proper washroom. They had to go in the bush or some time when they stopped to eat or drink tea. There were public washrooms but women did not want to use this type of washroom. Most of the time they had no choice. Next morning, when Mahesh woke up, he went outside for some fresh air. Oh my God, there was an open sewer system, he ran back in the hotel. He couldn't take the smell. When the driver came with the tempo, they had to run to the tempo. They went on a boat ride in open sea to watch dolphins. It made them feel good, the sea water and beaches were very clean and nice. The white sand looked nice and the sea food was very delicious. After spending two days in Goa, the driver drove them back to Gujarat. Same story, they drove all day and night, without nice food or washroom. Goa trip was very nice, but Mahesh would fly next time. They spent more time on the highway than seeing the sights.

Most of the time they were in the Gujarat. People of Gujarat are very friendly. They talked to Mahesh all the time. One day Mahesh saw one man biting his dog. Mahesh asked him why he bit his dog. The man replied that this dog bit ten of his friends and relatives, but never bit or barked at his mother-in-law. She has been there for the last two weeks. Mahesh laughed so hard and asked him to please leave his dog alone. One day, Mahesh and Bijma went for a walk in the rural area. It was a very hot day and they saw two small kids playing in the sand and one baby sleeping in hot sun. Their mom was working in the building as a labourer, carrying mixed concrete to the top of the building.

Mahesh asked Bijma if she saw any shops close by. She said yes and they went to the shop and bought some clothes, cookies, toys, and cold drinks for the kids. Mahesh went to the kids and sat down with them and started playing and feeding the kids. His wife asked him what was he was doing? She told him to give the food and clothes to them and go. Mahesh replied to Bijma, that she does not understand. This is how he was brought up. His mom had also left him like this when he was a baby and worked the farm. Mahesh spent more than one hour with these kids.

After hearing this, Bijma wanted to donate some food to the poor people. They went to the village to find out where the best place to donate would be. They went to a temple nearby and talked to the pandit (priest). The pandit suggested that instead of giving food, they could pay for the poor boys and girls wedding expenses. They had eleven boys and eleven girls waiting to get married. The pandit told them that they are looking for donations because they did not have money. Mahesh asked the pundit if they do not have any money to get married, why do they want to get married. However, Bijma agreed to pay for all the expenses. It only cost her one thousand Canadian dollars, because pundit and mandir were free from the organization. This was the first time they saw eleven weddings at the same time with one pundit performing the wedding. The organizing committee gave Mahesh and Bijma a lot of respect and honoured Mahesh with a beautiful shawl.

Taking Risks

Mahesh had always took many risks in his life, like changing flat tires on the highway. One day he went to see a client on a cold call, this is when you meet a client that you haven't met before. The prospect was multi-millionaire, living in the countryside, three hours from his office. Before Mahesh left his office, he called and confirmed. The client, Mr. Sheik, sounded like he was a mature man in his fifties. When Mahesh arrived at the address, he rang the bell. One young lady opened the door. Mahesh asked her where her father? The lady just stared at him. Mahesh said, "Mr. Sheik", the lady replied, "He is my husband, he will be home soon, come inside." Mahesh asked her if he can use the washroom. She said of course. When Mahesh went in the washroom, he heard something that sounded like grinding teeth. When he looked back, there was a German Shepherd in the washroom. Mr. Sheik kept this dog in the washroom, so when Mahesh came, he would be safe. When Mahesh was in the washroom, the young lady realized about the dog, she came in the washroom to protect him.

She told Mahesh not to move, just finish quickly, and get out of here. As soon as they came out from the washroom, her husband came in the house with a twelve-gauge rifle in his hand, watching Mahesh pulling his zipper and cleaning his pants. He asked what was going on? Before Mahesh could say anything, Mr. Sheik said, "I will forgive you, but the one up there will not forgive you", he pointed his finger up. Mahesh thought Mr. Sheik meant his God, Allah and felt relieved. Mahesh was not worried about Allah. Mr. Sheik pointed up again and said to him, "They will not forgive you." When Mahesh looked up there were two huge German Shepherds looking down at him. Mahesh looked at the woman, she did not say anything. Mahesh grabbed his laptop and ran to his car.

The whole time he was driving to this client's house, he kept thinking, today will be good for business because he knew his prospect was a wealthy man.

Mahesh had gone through all of this, but he was not afraid of taking risks again. In India, with the first rickshaw ride, he could have ended up murdered, tempo driving at night on the Khandara Mountain, and riding on a camel without any safety.

Akshay wanted to take them to Mount Abu to see the sunset. He told Mahesh, it is a very nice scene. It looks like the sun is going down very close to you. Next day, they all went to see the sun set on Mount Abu. It was a one-day drive on the mountain, narrow roads, sharp bends all over, and the sign said "Kharnak more" in Hindi. Dangerous bend, drive carefully. It really was very dangerous bend with no guards. If you miss one turn, you're dead. They say if the van goes down, no one will survive and no one will go there to look for you. When they reached the top of the mountain, the sun had already set. They went to a temple right on the top of the mountain, needed to go on a gondola lift. It was a very scary ride with no safety belt, but was fun. They spent the night in the hotel. It was very cold, no hot water in the hotel. The manager gave them hot water in buckets for a bath. At the end, they returned home safely.

Taj Mahal

They hired the same tempo and driver again to Agra. They visited the Taj Mahal. It was a very nice design, clean inside and outside with its colour changing from white in the daytime and to yellow during a full moon. After seeing Taj Mahal, the guide showed them the finest Mughal fort of India. The Agra foods are very delicious especially Bidaai/kachori and Jalebi. And from Agra they drove to Delhi City. Delhi city is another famous city of India. The guide took everyone to India Gate. After lunch the guide told Mahesh the next stop is Jantar Mantar. Mahesh asked the guide about Jantar Mantar. "Is it something like black magic?" He said, "No, you all will like this very much."

Jantar Mantar is located in the modern city of New Delhi. It consists of nineteen architectural astronomy instruments. The site was one of five built by Maharaja Jai Singh of Jaipur, it was very interesting thing to see. To learn more about Jantar Mantar they needed more time, but sadly, they had to leave. Then they went to see the Samadhi of Bapu. It was surrounded by a beautiful garden. The whole area was well maintained by the Indian government.

Posing in front of the Taj Mahal.

Before the driver left for Haridwar, for overnight, he stopped in Vrindavan. Vrindavan is a holy town of Uttar Pradesh, Northern India. The Hindu deity Krishna was said to have spent his childhood there. The guide handed over his group to one of the priests, who first took everyone to a place where he said that Krishna was rolling around in his childhood and encouraged everyone to roll around too. It was sand, so it easy to roll. After rolling for about ten minutes, he asked everyone to join him inside the Banke Bihari Temple.

Rolling around in the sand

The priest started to pray for everyone and asked for donations. Everyone in the group stopped for the prayer, gave a small donation, and then stood to the side. The priest saw Mahesh had $20 in his gift plate with some fruit and sweets. $20 Canadian is Indian 1000 rps. The priest thought Mahesh would give in to his demands. Mahesh was given three options: first 35000 rps; second 45000 rps; and third 55000 rps. The priest said to Mahesh his prayer will bring good life to his family. He asked Mahesh's grandfather's father's name.

Mahesh said, "I don't know."

Priest, "Your grandmother's name?"

Mahesh, "I don't know"

Priest, "It's okay, your father's name?"

Then the priest asked Mahesh to say all his kids' names. This will give them a good education.

Mahesh said, "They already have completed school"

The Priest replied, "They will get married soon."

Mahesh, "They're all married."

Priest, "They will get a nice job."

Mahesh, "They all have nice jobs."

Then the priest asked Mahesh to repeat after him, "I am promising in front of Krishna that I will give donation for 35,000 rps to the priest"

Mahesh responded, "I am promising in front of mighty God Lord Krishna that I am giving 1,000 rps to the priest instead of 35000 rps."

Everyone started laughing. Akshay thought Mahesh would end up giving a lot of money to the priest. When they came back to their tempo, Mahesh's daughter's father-in-law got mad at the guide and told him that he was not needed anymore and fired him without pay. But Mahesh paid him before asking him to leave. Mahesh was the one who dealt with payments. It was always more fun and safe when you travel with Mahesh.

The next day, they went to Haridwar, an ancient city and municipality in the Haridwar district of Uttarakhand. According to a Hindu legend, it was here that goddess Ganga was released into a mighty river from a lock of Lord Shiva's hair. They had prayers every evening at the Ganga River, also named as Ganges River. This is the biggest river in India. They believed this is a holy river. Mahesh and Bijma did their prayer, and bathed in the river. Haridwar priest and people say if you bathe in this river, all of your sins will wash away. The water was very cold but they wanted to get rid of their sins. Mahesh and Bijma dove in the cold river but they could not stay for long. They could not wash away all their sins.

Mahesh and Bijma washing away *most* of their sins.

After two days in Haridwar, the tempo left for Gujarat. They drove through the state of Rajasthan. Most of the crimes that happen on India's Highway are in Rajasthan. They stopped for one night in a small city. The hotel had no hot water system. They bathe in cold water. For dinner there was a restaurant not very far from their hotel, a very nice place. They served dinner with open air dance and live music. Mahesh and Bijma decided to have their dinner in this restaurant. They went there and started drinking beer and dancing. Mahesh started dancing with the performer. Mahesh did not know if the dancer was a he or a she. This person was dancing with six pots on their head. Mahesh started dancing beside him and bumped the dancer hard with his hip. All the pots fell on top of them and they both fell down.

Everyone thought this was going to be big trouble. Good thing Mahesh knew how to manage these types of problems. Mahesh started laughing and bought everyone a drink and made them his friends. The owner of the restaurant became his friend as well. It was fun for everyone and they all enjoyed their dinner.

**Dancing in Rajasthan. Photo taken
right before the pots fell.**

When they were ready to go back to the hotel, it was late at night. They started walking but the owner of the restaurant stopped them. He told Mahesh not to walk back. The owner offered to call a cab or have his staff go with him. Mahesh said it was not too far and they will be okay.

The owner insisted but Mahesh did not accept the offer. They started walking to their hotel, some looters were following them. Good thing the restaurant owner called the cops for their protection. The police officer came to the hotel and said good thing the restaurant owner called for your protection. The cops informed them they were being followed by some looters. Mahesh believed the policeman and gave him some tip, which made them happy. He asked the hotel manager if the policemen were telling the truth. The manager told Mahesh, people have to be very careful in this area.

Traditional clothing of Rajasthan

The daytime driving was so nice. For lunch, they stopped at a dhaba for some food. Dhaba is the best fast food you can get on the highway. And they went to a city called Surat. Surat is known for silk weaving. Saris are very cheaply found in this city. The ladies did a lot of shopping. They were very pleased with the driver for stopping in this city. After shopping in Surat, they visited some temples. Temples are all over on the highway. Every ten minutes of driving you can see a big temple. Sometimes they stopped for lunch because the food is very cheap and delicious in the temples. Some of the temple did not charge for food, but you can give some donations.

In India, five weeks went by fast. Most of the time they were driving on the highway. In big cities like Mumbai and Delhi, they were always stuck in traffic. Mahesh had never seen traffic like in Mumbai before in his life. Cows, rickshaws, motorcycles, bikes, and people on the road at the same time. Sometimes the cars came in opposite direction and blowing their horn. Mumbai is the capital city of the India state of Maharashtra, it is the most popular city in India.

One time Mahesh and his wife crossed the road for some coconut water. After drinking the coconut water, they wanted to come back to the tempo. They could not cross the road. They tried so many times but it was very busy. Akshay was watching them. After watching for sometime, he realised that they could not cross. He walked over and held their hand to help them cross safely to the other side. He told them to keep walking, the drivers will stop for them. If they waited for the drivers to stop, they will not stop. They were very worried while they crossed the road. After they crossed, the guide took them to a food market on a beach. It had lots of dhabas in one location. It was hard to decide what to eat.

When it was time to fly back to Canada, everyone was very sad to part ways. The host asked them to come back to India during the Diwali Festival time. It was a very memorable trip. They learned a lot of new things and luckily no one got sick. They ate lots of different types of healthy food and most of the time they only drank bottled water. Driving was very dangerous, but no accidents. Vacationing in India needed more than five weeks.

Mahesh wanted to find out what village his family came from. It was very difficult after so many years to locate the exact location. Akshay promised Mahesh, when next he visits, Akshay will take him to the village where his caste of people were mostly from. It is in Lucknow, Uttar Pradesh.

South Pacific Trip

Now that he was back at work, it took some time for business to pick up again. For him, it was not very difficult because Mahesh is hardworking, honest and committed to his clients. The commissions are very good so he liked to do this type of business. Mahesh was never scared to go and meet his clients in new areas, at night or in dangerous apartments, because he knew how to deal with people, and how to help them with their financial future. Most of his clients liked him; they gave referrals to their families and friends. Most of his business was from referrals. Mahesh's family always wondered where Mahesh got the money for all the vacations he went on.

Mahesh was on vacation most of the time and usually out of the country. He was never scared to take loans or increase the credit limits on his card. His credit cards are always full. Bijma would worry all the time about how Mahesh would pay all the loans and credit cards. Mahesh had a lot of confidence in his business. He will bring the business to upper level and he always has a good credit record. In a very short time, he managed to pay off all of his credit cards and loans.

In July 2017, his eldest daughter, Kitty, and son-in-law, Navin, wanted him to go on a vacation with them. She had been planning this vacation for more than five years. She wanted to go to New Zealand, Australia and Fiji Islands. Mahesh could not say no to them because their kids were very much attached to him and Bijma. Mahesh and Bijma were staying with Kitty when they were born. So, Mahesh and his wife arranged for a three weeks holiday again, to go on a vacation to New Zealand, Australia, and Fiji Islands with Kitty, Navin and their grandkids.

Part 1: New Zealand "We're going on an Adventure"

Matamata

Mahesh, Bijma, Kitty, Navin, and two grandkids, Lucian and Chyah, all six of them were ready to fly to Auckland, New Zealand. They were very much excited for this holiday. They had picked July because it was during their summer holidays. However, in the South Pacific, it was "winter". They flew from Toronto to Vancouver, then from Vancouver to Auckland. They arrived at the Auckland airport very early in the morning. They decided to rent a seven-passenger van and headed to Matamata, home to Middle Earth. This was one of the locations the very famous Lord of the Rings movie trilogy was filmed.

The Hobbiton

Kitty, Navin and grandkids had seen all the movies. They watch this movie every Christmas season. They were very excited to see this location. When the tour guide asked who has seen the movies, they all jumped up and responded they had seen all the movies. When the guide asked about a particular scene, Navin knew the lines exactly, "I am going on an adventure" and won the opportunity to reenact the scene. The guide was shocked, everyone clapped for him and Kitty forgot to video record the scene.

They visited every hobbit home and took a lot of pictures. The guide talked about a tree made by men. They used it in the film; you cannot tell that it is artificial. The director spent a lot of money on this tree, but it was only a few seconds in the movie. Now what Mahesh really wanted was a nice cold beer.

At the end, the guide took everyone to "The Green Dragon", a bar frequented by the hobbits. Mahesh only had one drink because he had to drive to Thermal Valley in Rotorua. Bijma wanted to visit Rotorua since she had learned about Rotorua in secondary school. She was very happy because her dream came true after so many years.

Grabbing a pint at Green Dragon

The people of New Zealand are very nice and helpful. When Mahesh inquired about Thermal Valley in Rotorua, they helped him book the hotel and gave the best direction to get there before dark. The receptionist gave them her cell phone number and the hotel's phone number for Mahesh to call if he get lost.

Driving from Matamata to Rotorua was a lot of fun. They did not have a navigation system in the van. All the driving was done by road map. Navin read the map and Mahesh drove. After missing a few times, they arrived at the hotel. The hotel did not look like a hotel building, it looked more like a residential house. It was very clean and safe. Next morning, they drove to the EcoThermal park, the famous Wai-o- Tapu Thermal Wonderland to see the Rotorua's hot springs, geothermal mud pool and redwood site.

After lunch, they drove to Mahesh's nephew's house in Auckland city. His nephew was the son of his manager from Industrial Marine Engineering Limited. Mahesh's manager was his second cousin's husband. It was dark when they arrived in Auckland. Mahesh had called his nephew few times for directions. Finally, his nephew had to pick them up from McDonalds close to the highway. Mahesh had not seen his nephew for more than thirty years but was able to recognize him right away. Next day, his nephew took one day off from his job and gave them a nice tour of Auckland city.

Auckland is a major city in the north of New Zealand's north island. Mahesh's nephew drove them to the iconic sky tower where you get a panoramic view of the city. Then they drove to the city's oldest park, Auckland Domain. It is based around an extinct volcano.

From New Zealand, they flew to Sydney, Australia to Mahesh brother's house. His brother and his daughter picked them from the airport. Mahesh has three brothers in Australia, one lives in Melbourne and the youngest one lives in Newcastle. They both came to Sydney to meet them. The brother who lived in Sydney is a builder. He builds residential houses for his clients. And as for himself, he is renting.

Part 2: Sydney Australia

Sydney is one of Australia's largest cities. It is best known for its Harbourfront Sydney Opera House.

Mahesh and his brother, Nawal, took everyone by boat to see the Sydney Opera House. They took lots of pictures, then had lunch at the Hard Rock Cafe. The food was very delicious. Australian beer is same as Fijian beer. In the evening everyone got together at Mahesh's brother's house for dinner. It was a very enjoyable night. They did all the cooking. They were all singing, dancing and drinking until morning. His brother had a nice karaoke set. Mahesh also sang, he only scored ten points out of hundred. However, Mahesh's grandson can sing very well.

A view of the Sydney Opera House

Next day, they all went for a train ride. The train ride was very smooth, seats are very comfortable, and you can turn the backrest from one side to the other. They stayed eight days in Australia. One day his younger brother, Jovan, took them to Newcastle, not very far from Sydney. Mahesh's brother is a pharmacist and owned a pharmacy. His wife, she is a doctor, they are very much settled in Australia.

Karaoke Time

Part 3: Fiji

After spending eight days in Sydney, they flew to Fiji via Wellington, New Zealand. They only had one hour to change planes. The flight attendant told them their luggage will go directly to Nadi, Fiji. When they were in Wellington airport, they saw their suitcases were on the conveyor belt. When they asked the immigration officer, the officer told them to grab all the luggage and join the line. When they talked to the flight attendant and explained they have an hour to catch their plane, she ran and spoke to the immigration and customs officers. The officers were very nice to them, gave them a chance to go in front of the line. The flight attendant and custom officer worked together, they told everyone except Navin, to run to the boarding area. He had to drop all the bags on the conveyor belt. All of them had to make a mad dash up the escalator and down a long winding corridor before reaching the boarding area. The officer told Navin that after he drops the bags on the belt, he has to run as fast as he can or else he will miss the flight and take the next one, maybe the next day. It was fun for everyone, except

Mahesh's wife, because she can't run as fast as everyone. Navin came after one minute, sweating in the air condition airport. And at the end they announced that the flight was delayed.

In Fiji, their hotel was booked across the airport. It was night when they arrived. Next day they took half day trip to a South Sea Island tour from Denarau Resort. It was a thirty-minute ferry ride. Everyone enjoyed the South Sea Island because the food and drinks were included. Kitty, Navin and the kids are outdoor people, who enjoyed the swimming and snorkeling. They all went in a Semi-Submersible coral viewer to see beautiful fish life, coral reef and a shark.

Next morning, Mahesh rented an eight-passenger van. Eight seater because they had a lot of luggage with them. They drove across the island to his brother's house in Korovou, Tailevu. Driving was fun for the kids with lots of speed humps. Most of the time they drove over the speed hump, hammering without slowing down. The kids in the back seat, bumping and laughing along. After a five-hour drive, they arrived at his brother Hara's house. This is the same house Mahesh paid to get built when he was working in Suva City, in Industrial Marine Engineering Limited. At this moment, Hara did some farming just to occupy the land. He had some coconut trees in his front yard. Mahesh's grandkids enjoyed picking their own coconut by themselves.

Next morning Hara came to him when he was sleeping and asked for the van key to go to Korovou market. Mahesh told him to wait for him. Hara did not want to wait or else he will be late. And if he's late, there won't be any hot peppers in the market. Mahesh laughed and handed over the key to him. Bijma asked him why he was laughing. Mahesh told her that she would not understand. But she insisted that he tell her. Mahesh took Bijma on the porch and he showed her all the land. Twelve acres of freehold land and all full of grass. He told her that when he was farming this land it was full of rice and vegetables. Mahesh supplied the vegetables to market vendors and his brother cannot even plant a pepper plant. He has to run early in the morning for fresh vegetables. Shame on him.

When his brother came back from the market, one of his cousins came with him. He is also a farmer, a dairy farmer. His land is adjacent to Mahesh's land. They dug the ground for lovo. Lovo is cooking the food under the ground on hot stone. Mahesh asked Navin to help, so he can learn how to do lovo cooking. Navin likes doing hard manual work and any outside activity. After they finished putting all the chicken and vegetables on the hot stone, they buried them. When Navin finished and came in the house, Mashesh asked him if he learned anything. Navin replied that they have wasted a lot of food. To this, Mahesh replied, wait one hour. After about an hour and a half, Mahesh's brother and cousin went back and got all the food out of the ground. Mahesh sent for Navin to help them again and to learn how it is done. The food was fully cooked and smelled nice. When Navin ate the food, he said it was delicious, not oily or too spicy. He asked Mahesh if they can do this in Toronto. Mahesh replied yes. Now that you know how to do lovo, the next time we rent a cottage, we will do lovo cooking in Toronto.

Digging a hole for lovo.

Next morning, they all decided to go to Suva City. Suva City is the capital, and largest city in Fiji. It is about one and a half hour drive from Tailevu. The first place they went was McDonald's for lunch. After lunch, Navin asked, how many hours before they arrive at Suva? Mahesh laughed, and said we are in Suva City, what do you think, there will be high rise buildings like in Toronto. From there they went to the museum and the historical garden. Navin wanted something as a souvenir to take back. Mahesh took him to the handicraft market because the museum was way overpriced.

At the handicraft market, Navin saw a nice crafted sword. The market vendor wanted $145 Canadian. Mahesh went and bargained it down. He bought it for only $40 because Mahesh can speak the Fijian language. Navin was surprised. And every time anyone needed to purchase, they came to him first. They spent all day in the city, shopping and viewing the sites. Next day, Mahesh showed them the place where he stayed when he first moved to Tailevu. He showed his grandkids how far he had to walk to school without shoes. That was about sixty years now and the road is still gravel. They drove to another small town, where Kitty went to school. Mahesh asked the principal for permission, to see the inside of the classrooms.

After spending three days in the eastern side of the island, the weather started changing. It started raining and looked like it will rain for a few more days. Mahesh told everyone to pack and go to the western side of the island. In Fiji western side mostly sunny weather. Mahesh asked his brother to come with his wife and stay in Denarau island for the rest of the holiday. In Denarau Island there are five major hotels, Mahesh booked his with Hilton Fiji. To get in Denarau Island, there's no boat ride necessary, it is a small private island, it is west of Viti Levu. During the night there was a fire walk show, Navin was invited to take part in grog drinking ceremony. Grog is a traditional drink of Fiji. After the ceremony they showed how to cook the food underground. This time it was done more professionally. It's called Lovo and the dinner was Lovo food also.

After the dinner there was great entertainment. Next day, most of the time they spent in the sea, playing and swimming. Hara was also there. He took the kids to the sugarcane farm, bought some sugar cane to chew. Hara had cut the cane in pieces for them to chew. Kids liked them very much. They liked their holiday in Fiji. Mahesh's, grandson asked him, "Why did you leave Fiji, it is very beautiful." Mahesh replied, "So that your mom can meet your dad."

Los Angeles

The next day at 9pm was their flight back to Toronto through Los Angeles. Kitty and her family flew from Los Angeles to Toronto. Mahesh and his wife stayed in the United States, at his cousin Master's house. Master requested that Bro also come and spend one week together with them. Bro was living in Vancouver, BC. They arrived one day before Mahesh. Both of Mahesh's cousins came to the airport an hour before to pick Mahesh and Bijma. Immigration officers held Mahesh for more than one hour. His cousins had been waiting for them for more than two hours. Finally, when Mahesh and Bijma came out they relaxed and were ecstatic to see them.

First thing in the morning, Mahesh rented an eight-passenger van, so everyone can travel together. Most of the time Mahesh did all the driving. There were six of them, his two cousins, and their wives. First place they end up that night was a Casino. To play the slot machines. In a casino there was not any self-parking, only valet parking. Mahesh, in his excitement, handed over the van key without checking the licence plate number. And all the documents were in the van. The valet driver gave him a slip, which Mahesh hand it over to his wife and then forgot about it.

When they were ready to leave, Mahesh could not find the slip and he did not know the licence plate number. Mahesh went to the security officer to get some help, they told him they have no control over this. The officer told Mahesh to talk to the person who parked his van. Mahesh could not recognize the person who he gave the key to. They all looked the same in their uniform. After some time, Bijma came laughing. Mahesh was very upset and asked her why she was laughing. She took out the slip and asked, "Is this what you all are looking for?" Oh my God, it was a big relief for Mahesh, and now they had something to talk about for the rest of the holiday.

Next morning, all three cousins went to a farm for goat, but they came with a duck. They had to clean the duck. Good thing the farmer killed the duck for them, but they had to clean the duck outside under a tree. It was a very hot day, they were drinking beer like water and the duck curry made a very nice lunch. In the night they went again to play the slots. This time a different Casino with self-parking. Mahesh parked the van by himself and marked the spot. They spent more than eight hours in the Casino. In Los Angeles four days passed by so quickly and now it was time to fly back to Toronto. They all had a very good time, because after a long time all his cousins have been together. At the time of departure, all of them were very emotional. Before leaving, Mahesh suggested to everyone, they should plan again, next year in Toronto, Canada.

After the holidays, Mahesh had to work hard, so he can make some money to cover all the expenses he acquired from his holiday, especially in the Casino. Mahesh became very diligent and started working very hard in Ontario and in Alberta. Mahesh qualified for all the campaigns in the year, (triple crown), and a major campaign. The Sun Life Financial company has this king of campaigns once a year, known as Conversion. It is a three-day trip to Punta Cana, Dominican Republic.

Young girl's Wedding

Mahesh and Bijma always liked to help people. They once helped a girl whom they did not know very well to get married. Her brother was opposed to her marriage and was treating her poorly. She was thrown out of her brother's house, and she did not have anywhere else to go. Mahesh and Bijma helped her out by giving her a place to stay, and arranged for her to get married to the boy she wanted to marry.

In the Fijian community it is customary that a bride be given away by her parents and family. Since this girl didn't have anyone, they took the role of her "parents" so that she can proceed with her marriage according to tradition. The wedding was done as a Hindu ceremony that Mahesh and his wife organized. The ceremony was well performed without any disturbances. There were rumours that the girl's brother would come and disrupt the wedding ceremony. As you know, Mahesh does not scare easily, but he asked his son-in-law Navin to attend the wedding, just in case.

It was important to Mahesh and his wife to help people who are in need, especially people who are from their community. They felt that helping others would lead to their own successes in life.

Punta Cana, Dominican Republic

After more successful months with Sun Life, Mahesh earned a trip to the Dominican Republic with Bijma. Mahesh and his wife were welcomed in red carpet ceremony at the Punta Cana Hard Rock Hotel and Casino.

Red Carpet in Punta Cana

It had thirteen luxurious pools with swim up bars and nine restaurants. Mahesh and Bijma stayed an extra day for the casino. One evening Mahesh and his wife went in the Casino when there was daylight outside, they ended up playing for a long time, it was after midnight when they decided to go back to their hotel room. When they came out of the Casino they could not figure out how to get back to their hotel room. There was no one around to ask.

They were walking in the dark without knowing if they are going in the right direction or not. Luckily, they saw a cart on the other side of a bridge. Mahesh called the driver for help. The cart driver asked what happened, and why are you two out so late. Mahesh told him that they were in the Casino, and when they went inside it was daylight. Mahesh gave him the address of their room, the driver laughed, and said this is far away from their hotel room, and that they were going in the wrong direction. The cart driver was laughing and asked if they at least won anything. Mahesh replied no, and his wife replied that she did, but not a big amount.

The next day the company organized a BBQ on the beach with a live band, delicious food and dancing on the beach. It was an enjoyable night with beautiful weather. There was a market outside on the beach also. Mahesh bought one bottle of their famous drink, Mamajuana; they said you could mix with water whenever you drink it. The taste and strength will remain the same forever.

Next morning after breakfast, Mahesh and Bijma went to the beach. It was very nice weather, they did some swimming, and then sat on the beach looking at the sea, watching the waves coming from the ocean. Mahesh was there for a long time, his wife asked what happened to him. Mahesh said nothing, then he asked her to sit down beside him and look at the waves.

He asked his wife, "How far can you see?"

She said, "Very far".

"Do you know what direction you are looking?"

"Yes, South."

Mahesh said "Yes, you are correct." Mahesh sat silently for a while. "Fiji is also south of here, these waves may be coming from Fiji, and ending up here. I am thinking about my dream. Actually, I feel I have achieved my dream. My dream was to have my own house, glass window office, parking spot for my car, and my own time to come, and go in the office, coffee in my hand. Just like these waves, they come all the way from the south and end up here. I have achieved my goal. This was my goal, but only one thing remains." Mahesh stands up. "I have to do some fishing. My dream was to catch a big fish, I mean a really big fish, bigger than myself."

Mahesh and Bijma went to the hotel lobby to inquire about deep-water fishing. They found a company called Island Routes Adventure Tours, and they were arranging deep water fishing. They were very serious about what they do. After speaking with the guide, and the captain of the Punta Cana Deep Sea Fishing Vessel, they insisted they knew the best spots to catch a big fish, but he needed at least five people, and no more than eight people to take the boat in the deep sea. The cost for a half day trip is five hundred dollars American. Mahesh asked his colleagues if they were interested in deep water fishing, four of them showed some interest, but one did not show up, so Mahesh asked his wife to join them and told everyone to be in the hotel lobby at 10am sharp the next morning.

In the morning when they arrived at the hotel lobby, the van was waiting for them. The van driver had to go and pick up more people for another boat as well. After driving for more than one hour, Mahesh asked his captain how long it will take before they arrive at the boat. The captain said not so long. The driver asked Mahesh "Why are you asking? Are you getting late?" Mahesh replied that they have a gala dinner this evening, they need to be back at the hotel before 6pm. They really did not want to miss this. They were told the gala dinner would be the best part of the vacation.

Finally, they reached the small boat which took them to the big fishing vessel. Mahesh's wife had difficulty getting in the big boat, finally she makes it with the help of one of the crew members. Everyone clapped for her. When they went into the deep ocean, the weather was very nice. The blue sea water looked so beautiful, the waves were a little high but not dangerous or difficult for fishing. The captain placed three fishing lines in the sea. The one in the middle, the captain asked Mahesh to look after.

The Captain caught few small fish. Mahesh was not here for small fish, so he went to the Captain and asked if he had any bait or could they cut this small fish for bait. The captain asked Mahesh "Where are you from? Have you done this kind of fishing before?" Mahesh answered that he is from the Fiji Islands, and has been fishing many times with his uncle and seen him fishing in the deep sea.

Then the captain said to him "That's why I was wondering why you looked so confident. Two of your colleagues are getting sea sick but you and your wife are doing okay." Then the captain said to him "Tell her go inside and stay there for a bit." He then asked a crew member to bring some bait for him, he said to Mahesh. "Be careful when you throw the bait." Mahesh threw the bait in the sea and released his fishing line another fifty feet. The captain was watching him the whole time, Mahesh know his line is so close to propeller.

Just after a short time Mahesh's line was moving out so fast. He yelled, "I got a catch!" The Captain knew this was a big fish. He quickly jumped up and held the line, telling a crew member to cut the engine off. He showed Mahesh how to control the fishing rod, Mahesh had never caught a big fish like this before. After controlling for more than one hour he asked one of his colleagues to help him. When captain saw how his colleague was handling the fishing rod, the captain asked Mahesh to take over he would lose the fish.

The captain was holding the grabber. Mahesh took the fishing rod and tried to bring the fish close to the boat so many times, as soon as the captain went to grab the fish, it goes back more than fifty feet away. Finally, Mahesh brought the fish very close to the boat, when he saw, he yelled loudly it's a shark. The captain and the crew member said to him it is not a shark, it's a white marlin. The captain told everyone to get inside the boat, his wife kept taking video from her phone. The captain yelled at Mahesh's wife to get inside. The captain said to Mahesh, "As soon as I bring the fish inside the boat you get inside quickly."

Mahesh brought the fish very close to the boat. The Captain used his grabber, and brought the fish in the boat very quickly, and started hammering with rubber hammer to keep the fish calm. Now everyone started taking photos, Mahesh's wife wanted to make a video, but the water was rough, so she went inside after she took some photos. One of Mahesh's colleagues sent the photo to the manager who was organizing the gala dinner and told him that they may be little late for dinner

Mahesh went to the Captain and requested to go back to our hotel as soon as possible. They did not need to take any fish. He told the captain that he can keep the fish, they just did not want to miss the gala dinner. So, the captain took them directly to the island, where the small boat was, and from the small boat to the van to take them to their hotel before 6pm. As soon as Mahesh and his colleagues arrived at the gala dinner, all the advisors start cheering and clapping, saying "The fishermen are here" and their photo was on the big screen, with the fish.

The Big Fish

Sun Life Financial is recognized as one of the best places to work in Ontario. The Gala was amazing, they had a lot of fun dancing until one am. The next day was their flight back to Toronto. Mahesh went back to work happily. Most of the time he worked from home. because he had achieved his goal. Some of his colleagues call him guru (guru is an Indian term for a person they respect and take advice from). They called Mahesh guru, because he is always helpful to everyone in the office, his family, and clients. Mahesh did not close his office door when he is in the office. Anyone who needed help, do not have to knock, just walk in. Sometimes they just come and talk to him for some advice. Most of the time Mahesh goes out for lunch with his colleagues, and joint calls (joint call is to go together on appointments). There was a new female advisor in his office; she always asked Mahesh to go with her to her appointments outside of the city, at night, or in the apartment buildings.

How Mahesh found success at Sun Life

Have an Agenda and stick to it... most of the time.

The process of creating an agenda in advance helps you determine what is actually needed in a meeting. Mahesh is a big believer in face-to-face meetings. Assuming the meeting is necessary, you should create an agenda, and not just in your head but on paper as well. It shows respect for the other participants. It is particularly important when preparing for your client meeting. You need your client's input before you get in the client's house. Umbrella theory, better to have it, and not need it, than to need it, and not have it.

When you arrive at your client's house, do not park on the driveway. Keep your eyes open, see the type of cars they have, how neat the house is inside, and outside.

Listening is more important than talking. During the presentation, stop and ask your clients questions. Another secret to presenting well is to respect everyone's time. Once a meeting is underway, the goal should be to make it as short as possible. Do not confuse the client. It is not necessary to ask for a referral in the middle of your presentation. Most of the time Mahesh did not need to ask for a referral at all. His presentation did that for him.

Tips for dealing with clients

Ask your client to have dinner with you, either the night before the meeting, or the evening after the conclusion. Assuming the client says yes, choose a restaurant that you know well, that will make your client feel both comfortable, and special. Mahesh was well versed in Sun Life's client relationship management system. It is a robust and dynamic system that allows you to run and grow your business. Successful businessmen and women, like Mahesh, know their numbers, and know where their profit comes from.

In the end, client service requires you to be flexible, open-minded and able to handle the unexpected with grace.

Hobbies

Mahesh's hobbies includes driving. Most of the time he and Bijma would go for long drives, mostly north. In Ontario, if you drive north in the summer, you feel like you are driving in Fiji. Beautiful farms, lakes, everything looks green. Next thing is Casino. Mahesh always goes to Casino to play slot machines. He mostly goes north of Toronto, so he would have both a long drive, and play slot machine. Sometimes he goes to watch MLS soccer in downtown Toronto. He also likes to watch (UEFA) Europa league soccer and world cup in television. Mahesh retired from playing soccer a long time ago.

Cottage in Bancroft

After Mahesh returned from India, Fiji Islands, New Zealand, Australia, and Punta Cana, he planned a family vacation. Vishal and Melissa had recently had a baby girl, Gia, and he wanted to spend quality time with his grandkids. Mahesh and his family decided to go north. Vishal rented a cottage in Bancroft, Ontario. Bancroft is a small, charming town about 3 hours North of Toronto.

Mahesh really enjoyed staying at this cottage as it was right on a lake, and he was able to spend most of his time fishing. Mahesh caught some Lake Trout, Smallmouth Bass and Perch on his first day. Lucian, Chyah, Anjali and Ria were all around 10-12 years old. They had a great time at this cottage, they got to play in the water with canoes, kayaks, and paddle boats. Gia, who was only seven months old, had a chance to be around her old cousins.

Mahesh's grandkids are very good swimmers. One of his granddaughters was in the kayak and fell in the deep lake. Mahesh and Bijma went to her in a canoe to help her. However, she said, "Nana and Nani please go away, I don't need help."

Then she swam all the way back to the dock. Mahesh was very proud to see that his grandkids kids could swim that well, because Mahesh also was a very good swimmer when he was young.

Next day Mahesh asked Navin if he wanted to do some lovo cooking, since he learned how to in Fiji. Navin agreed and did it exactly how a lovo was meant to be done. First, he made a fire to heat the stones, then placed the food on the heated stones, and buried the foods for two hours. After two hours when he took the food out, it was cooked nicely. The food was cooked like how professionals do lovo. Three days went so fast, it was very nice. Everyone liked the lovo food, swimming in the lake, paddling canoes, kayaks and paddle boats.

This trip was very fun and everyone decided that it would become a tradition for the family to do a trip like this every year.

Retirement

Finally, Mahesh sent a letter to his financial centre manager, as follows:

Please be advised that effective April 26, 2018, I have decided to retire from the advisor role. I would like to thank the management, advisors, and staff members for all the support, and help during my thirteen years of employment with this company. Please be advised that my decision is final, I want to take a role for second level to spend my time with my family.

As soon as Mahesh's financial centre manager received the letter, he came into Mahesh's office, looking for him. He said, "What is this? Am I dreaming, is this is true?"

Mahesh replied, "This is not a dream, I have decided to move to the second level, to spend more time with my family. I have no complaints with management or with the company."

One of his best friends and colleagues, the one who would always call him guru, was shocked when he heard from the financial centre manager that Mahesh was retiring. He quickly came in to his office, and said to Mahesh "Guru, is what I am hearing from the financial centre manager, is he kidding to me or it is true? Did you give him a retirement letter?"

Mahesh said to him, "Yes, it is not a joke." His friend sat in his office for a long time, then says, "Can I go and talk to the financial center manager to ignore the letter or extend it to the end of the year?" Mahesh replied, "It is too late, I have made my decision."

The next day, the financial centre manager sent an email - Retirement - Mahesh Raj.

Please be advised that effective April 26, 2018 Mahesh Raj has decided to retire from his advisor role. Mahesh has provided many years of dedicated service to his advisors since joining our company in July of 2004. Mahesh recently attended his last convention just over two years ago showing his true commitment to excellence as an advisor. For those of you do not know Mahesh that well, Mahesh has been a very hard working and dedicated worker all of his life. Originating in his home country of Fiji Islands, Mahesh Started work at a very early age of 14, on a poultry farm, due to a family illness at the time. Mahesh was not able to complete his formal schooling, as he had to work, and help support the family. Mahesh was a very industrious and motivated man as his transition to real estate sales in the area of commercial land development. As mentioned even though he did not complete his formal education he took industry courses to learn the real estate trade. His next stop was in a number of sales and marketing roles in the area of industrial supplies. In order to further in his area he again took industry courses to improve his knowledge and skills.

Then, in 1987, as the country of Fiji was experiencing a number of political challenges, Mahesh decided to move his family to Canada to start a new life. And for fifteen years Mahesh spend time with Canada Post in the area of supervisor and parcel expediter applying his years of work experience from Fiji.

The final stop in his career journey has taken the next step after years of taking care of his clients. While Mahesh is a very quiet person, he has always been dedicated to work for his clients. He possesses a soft and determined passion to succeed in anything how dose. Mahesh is excited to spend more time with his family, and he plans to write a book, his autobiography as an example to what determination, perseverance and passion can produce as young boy, uneducated, refugee to a successful Canadian businessman.

Acknowledgements

The personal stories that appear in this book have been gathered over many years from a variety of sources. Although my memory has been pretty good, I received help and support from many family members to ensure these stories are accurate as possible.

These stories show how much I had to work and support my family, but also shows how my family, friends, community, neighbours and even strangers have made an impact on how I view what success is, and what is required to achieve it.

I came into this world with a very small chance of survival. Throughout my childhood and early life we relied on a lot of people to help me and my family survive. I was a poor boy from the Fiji Islands, with no education. When I was a child, it seemed like fishing and farming were my future.

Seeing successful people around me, and getting their advice over the years was a major motivator for me to break that cycle.

I started my career in a number of sales and marketing roles in the area of industrial supplies. In order to further my career in this area, I took industrial courses to improve my knowledge and skills. Then I went into real estate sales in the area of farmland development. As mentioned even though I did not complete formal education, I took courses to learn the real estate trade.

Then in 1987, I decided to move with my family to start a new life in Canada. Fiji was experiencing a number of political challenges, and had to do what was best for us, with the help of family and friends.

In 2018, I was excited to retire and spend more time with my family, and wanted to write a book, as an example to what determination, perseverance and passion can produce. An uneducated refugee became a successful Canadian Businessman.

I would like to thank everyone who has read this book for taking their time to get to know my story, and learn from my mistakes and successes. I have received a lot of praise for this endeavour, which makes me very proud and thankful for the people in my life.

I would also like to thank my children and their spouses for their help in editing and developing this book with me. Last but definitely not least, I would like to thank my wife Bijma, for believing in me and motivating me throughout my life and with writing this book. We have come a very long way together, and could not have gone this far without her.

Mahesh's family, 2019.

Index

MAHESH P. RAJ - AUTHOR

Printed in the United States
By Bookmasters